OECD *Economic Surveys*
Electronic Books

The OECD, recognising the strategic role of electronic publishing, will be issuing the OECD **Economic Surveys**, both for the Member countries and for countries of Central and Eastern Europe covered by the Organisation's Centre for Co-operation with Economies in Transition, as electronic books with effect from the 1994/1995 series -- incorporating the text, tables and figures of the printed version. The information will appear on screen in an identical format, including the use of colour in graphs.

The electronic book, which retains the quality and readability of the printed version throughout, will enable readers to take advantage of the new tools that the ACROBAT software (included on the diskette) provides by offering the following benefits:

- ❑ User-friendly and intuitive interface
- ❑ Comprehensive index for rapid text retrieval, including a table of contents, as well as a list of numbered tables and figures
- ❑ Rapid browse and search facilities
- ❑ Zoom facility for magnifying graphics or for increasing page size for easy readability
- ❑ Cut and paste capabilities
- ❑ Printing facility
- ❑ Reduced volume for easy filing/portability

Working environment: DOS, Windows or Macintosh.

Subscription:	FF 1 800	US$317	£200	DM 545
Single issue:	FF 130	US$24	£14	DM 40

Complete 1994/1995 series on CD-ROM:

FF 2 000	US$365	£220	DM 600

Please send your order to OECD Electronic Editions or, preferably, to the Centre or bookshop with whom you placed your initial order for this Economic Survey.

OECD
ECONOMIC
SURVEYS

1994-1995

IRELAND

ORGANISATION FOR ECONOMIC CO-OPERATION AND DEVELOPMENT

ORGANISATION FOR ECONOMIC CO-OPERATION AND DEVELOPMENT

Pursuant to Article 1 of the Convention signed in Paris on 14th December 1960, and which came into force on 30th September 1961, the Organisation for Economic Co-operation and Development (OECD) shall promote policies designed:

— to achieve the highest sustainable economic growth and employment and a rising standard of living in Member countries, while maintaining financial stability, and thus to contribute to the development of the world economy;

— to contribute to sound economic expansion in Member as well as non-member countries in the process of economic development; and

— to contribute to the expansion of world trade on a multilateral, non-discriminatory basis in accordance with international obligations.

The original Member countries of the OECD are Austria, Belgium, Canada, Denmark, France, Germany, Greece, Iceland, Ireland, Italy, Luxembourg, the Netherlands, Norway, Portugal, Spain, Sweden, Switzerland, Turkey, the United Kingdom and the United States. The following countries became Members subsequently through accession at the dates indicated hereafter: Japan (28th April 1964), Finland (28th January 1969), Australia (7th June 1971), New Zealand (29th May 1973) and Mexico (18th May 1994). The Commission of the European Communities takes part in the work of the OECD (Article 13 of the OECD Convention).

Publié également en français.

Table of contents

Box

Tables

Diagrams

BASIC STATISTICS OF IRELAND

THE LAND

Area (thousand sq. km)	70	Population of major cities, 1991 census (thousands)	
Agricultural area, 1991, as per cent of total area	62	Dublin (county and Co. Borough)	1 025
		Cork, Co. Borough	127
		Limerick, Co. Borough	52

THE PEOPLE

Population (April 1993)	3 563 000	Net emigration:	
Number of inhabitants per sq. km	51	Annual average 1987-1993	19 670
Increase in population: annual average 1987-1993	3 500	Annual average per thousand of population	5.6
Natural increase in population:		Labour force, total, April 1993	1 375 000
annual average 1987-1993	21 600	Civilian employment in:	
		Agriculture, forestry and fishing	144 000
		Industry and construction	312 000
		Other sectors	690 000

THE GOVERNMENT

Public current expenditure on goods and services, 1992 (as per cent of GNP)	20	Composition of Parliament (1994):	Seats
		Fianna Fail	67
Current government revenue, 1993 (as per cent of GNP)	36	Fine Gael	46
		Labour	32
Public debt, 31 December 1993 (as per cent of GNP)	109	Progessive Democrats	8
		Democratic Left	5
		Others	6
		Last general election: December 1994	

FOREIGN TRADE

Exports:		Imports:	
Exports of goods and services, as per cent of GNP (1993)	77	Imports of goods and services, as per cent of GNP (1993)	61
Main exports, 1993 (per cent of total):		Main imports, 1993 (per cent of total):	
Machinery and electrical goods	29	Machinery and electrical goods	37
of which:		Petroleum, petroleum products and related materials	4
Office machinery and data processing equipment	18	Textile manufactures	2
Meat and meat preparations	6	Iron and steel	1
Dairy products and birds' eggs	4	Clothing and footwear	5
Textile manufactures	2	Main suppliers, 1993 (per cent of total):	
Live animals chiefly for food	1	United Kingdom	36
Clothing and footwear	2	Other, European Union	20
Beverages	2	United States	17
Organic chemicals	9		
Medicinal and pharmaceutical products	5		
Main customers, 1993 (per cent of total):			
United Kingdom	28		
Other, European Union	40		
United States	9		

THE CURRENCY

Monetary unit: Irish pound	Currency unit per US dollar, average of daily figures:	
	Year 1994	0.67
	March 1995	0.63

Note: An international comparison of certain basic statistics is given in an annex table.

Introduction

With GNP growth of around 4 per cent in 1993 and over 5 per cent in 1994, Ireland remained the fastest-growing economy in the European Union. The expansion of output in 1993 was led by buoyant exports despite depressed conditions in continental Europe. Domestic demand, however, was damped by exceptionally high and volatile domestic interest rates during the exchange-rate crisis associated with the currency turbulence within the EMS at the end of 1992. The 10 per cent devaluation of the Irish pound in early 1993, though, removed such exchange and interest rate pressure, thus allowing a significant improvement in confidence. This resulted in a more balanced expansion in 1994, with personal consumption and business investment adding to continued strong export growth. Since the exchange rate has remained broadly stable in effective terms, despite the devaluation, inflation stayed low, aided by continued wage moderation and the subsequent gradual appreciation of the Irish pound against sterling. Output growth is expected to continue at about 5 per cent in both 1995 and 1996, supported by personal consumption and business investment.

Despite its good growth performance, the Irish economy continues to face high levels of public debt and unemployment. Buoyant tax revenues and the fall in debt interest payments kept the general government deficit at about 2 per cent of GDP in 1994. Consequently, there has been a significant decline in the debt-to-GDP ratio to 90 per cent. Tighter control on public expenditure appears to be necessary in order to sustain progress in reducing this ratio as specified in the Maastricht Treaty and to make room for a further reduction in the tax burden.

Rapid growth resulted in significant employment gains in 1994 that helped reduce the unemployment rate to 14½ per cent. To ensure a further decline in this rate, still the third highest in the OECD area, initiatives designed to increase the incentives to work have been taken in the context of both the 1994 and 1995

1

budgets. In addition, the high level of unemployment among poorly-educated people has generated interest in reform of education and training to improve employment opportunities.

Part I examines recent trends in both 1993 and 1994 and discusses the short-term outlook. This is followed by a review of monetary and fiscal policies in Part II. Part III analyses the recent progress in structural reform and is supplemented, in Part IV, by a special study of the Irish education and training system, including recent changes proposed by the government. Conclusions arising from the analysis in the Survey are presented in Part V.

I. Recent trends and prospects

Avoiding the recession

Since 1991, Ireland has recorded the fastest expansion of any country in the European Union (EU). While economic growth was negative in the EU in 1993, Ireland's GNP increased by 3.8 per cent (Diagram 1 and Box). Industrial output expanded at an even faster pace, in contrast to the declines experienced in many other European countries. While employment also fell in the EU in 1993, the growth of output in Ireland generated significant job gains. Such an outstanding performance of the Irish economy during a period of recession in Europe reflected its competitive strength. Indeed, despite the depressed conditions in continental Europe, export volume increased by 10 per cent during 1993, aided by the early recovery in the United Kingdom, Ireland's major market. The employment response was limited as domestic demand remained subdued in the wake of the currency crisis at the end of 1992, with exceptionally high and volatile interest rates depressing household and business sector confidence (Diagram 2).

The decline in interest rates in the first half of 1993 resulted in a recovery of personal consumption and business fixed investment in the second half of the year that continued into 1994, leading to a more broad-based expansion. Consequently, domestic demand was the major source of growth in 1994, while net exports made a smaller, though still positive, contribution. The continued rise in employment contributed to a decline in Ireland's high unemployment rate in 1994

3

Diagram 1. **OUTPUT AND EMPLOYMENT**

Percentage change

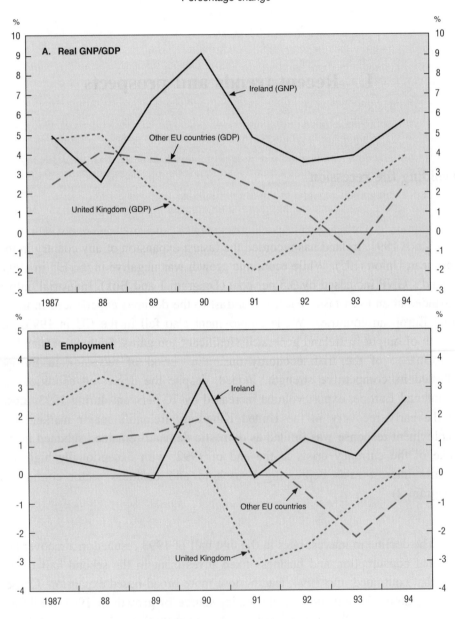

Source: OECD.

Box. GNP and GDP contrasted

In this survey GNP, rather than GDP, is consistently used as a measure of economic activity in Ireland as it shows the income and production that accrues to the country rather than the value of production within the geographical limits of Ireland. For most countries, there is little difference between GNP and GDP since income arising outside is balanced by the income of foreigners earned inside. In the case of Ireland, though, two factors make for a large difference between the income accruing to nationals and the value of domestic production. *First,* a series of current-account deficits during the 1970s and early 1980s led to an accumulation of foreign debt mainly incurred by the government sector with consequent debt service outflows. Net of other trading and investment income, these interest payments have averaged 2 per cent of GDP over the period 1987 to 1993. *Secondly,* the successful policy of transforming manufacturing industry by attracting foreign companies naturally involves a significant outflow of royalties and profits from this sector averaging 9 per cent of GDP over the same period (Table 1). As a result, overall GNP has been 11 per cent lower than GDP. In addition, GNP has also grown less rapidly than GDP, with real GNP expanding by 4 per cent annually between 1987 and 1994 against 4½ per cent for GDP.

Table 1. **A comparison of GNP and GDP**

	Growth in output (per cent)		Net property income payments (percentage points of GDP)		
	GDP	GNP	Profits, dividends and royalties repatriated from Ireland	Net interest and other	Total
1988	4.7	2.8	9.2	2.5	11.7
1989	6.6	5.6	10.1	2.6	12.7
1990	6.4	6.5	9.3	2.3	11.6
1991	1.3	2.8	8.4	1.8	10.2
1992	4.0	2.0	9.6	1.4	11.0
1993	4.1	3.8	10.4	1.2	11.6
Average	4.5	3.9	9.5	1.9	11.5

Source: National Income and Expenditure.

The composition of the difference between GNP and GDP has been changing in recent years. Since 1987, the swing into current-account surplus (despite these outflows) has led to an increase in private sector assets held abroad which has meant that the flow of net interest payments has fallen to 1¼ per cent of GDP. On the other hand, outflows of profits and royalties have risen to 10½ per cent of GDP, though fluctuating considerably from year to year. When Ireland, along with most other EU countries, moves to using the

(continued on next page)

(continued)

national accounts definitions adopted by the UN and OECD, together with current account definitions used by the IMF, the gap between GNP and GDP may change further (though marginally) as GNP will be lowered by the deduction of the unrepatriated profits of foreign companies but raised by the addition of the unrepatriated profits of Irish companies abroad. Such a change may lessen the differences in the year-to-year growth of GDP and GNP since, by using the IMF current account definitions, any differences in timing between earning and repatriating profits would not come into play.

The presence of dynamic foreign companies in certain high technology areas of manufacturing industry means that usual measures of international competitiveness are biased for Ireland. The activity of foreign companies is concentrated in five areas – computers, pharmaceuticals, medical technology, electrical engineering and other food where the principal activity is the production of soft drink concentrates. These industries represent the "modern" sector of the economy accounting for nearly 70 per cent of the net output of the foreign-owned manufacturing companies. This sector has a high level of productivity, with value added per employee being almost two and a half times higher than in the remainder of manufacturing (Table 2). As a result, in 1990, although the modern part of the economy accounted for only 28 per cent of industrial employment, it represented 48 per cent of value added and nearly 60 per cent of the gross operating surplus. This performance has been achieved with a markedly higher level of investment per employee than that seen in traditional industry, though, in 1990, the share of investment in output was lower. The increasing share of the "modern" sector in total employment has pushed the overall level of labour productivity in manufacturing (used to calculate unit labour costs) towards that of the modern sector. In addition, this sector has itself experienced rapid productivity growth. Consequently, measures of international competitiveness for Ireland have to take into account the dual nature of the manufacturing sector. High productivity growth in the modern sector does not improve competitiveness in the traditional sector. Consequently, for the manufacturing industry as a whole, competitiveness measures have to be based on relative movements of wages.

Table 2. **Manufacturing sector value added per employee**

Constant 1990 prices

	Level (Irf 000)[1]			Growth rates (3-year average, per cent)		
	Modern	Traditional	Total	Modern	Traditional	Total
1987	59.5	28.0	35.4			
1990	74.3	31.9	43.9	7.7	4.4	7.5
1993	91.3	33.6	53.0	7.1	1.7	6.5
Average 1987-93	76.6	31.3	44.4	7.4	3.1	7.0

1. In enterprises with more than 19 employees.
Source: Census of Industrial Production 1990, ESRI, CSO.

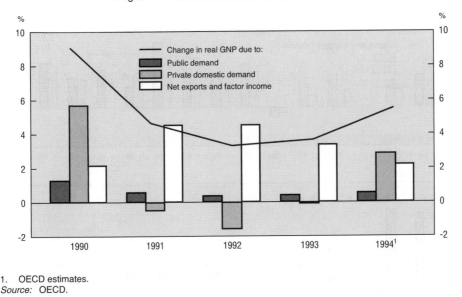

Diagram 2. **CONTRIBUTIONS TO GNP GROWTH**

Change in real GNP due to:
Public demand
Private domestic demand
Net exports and factor income

1. OECD estimates.
Source: OECD.

(Diagram 3). Inflation, which had accelerated somewhat during 1993, stabilised at about 2½ per cent in 1994.

The paragraphs below review, in more detail, the major economic developments since early 1993. This is followed by a discussion of short and medium-term projections for the Irish economy.

Strong exports lead growth...

The expansion of exports was responsible for most of the output growth in 1993 (Table 1). The effect on trade flows of the devaluation of the central rate of the Irish pound in the ERM by 10 per cent in January 1993, however, was modest since the effective depreciation of the currency proved to be much less over the period 1992 to 1994. The greater part of the decline of the exchange rate in 1993 was a reversal of the effective rise that had occurred following the exit of the UK currency from the ERM in September 1992. Compared with the first half of 1992, the effective rate of the Irish pound had fallen by only 4.2 per cent by

Diagram 3. **MACROECONOMIC PERFORMANCE**

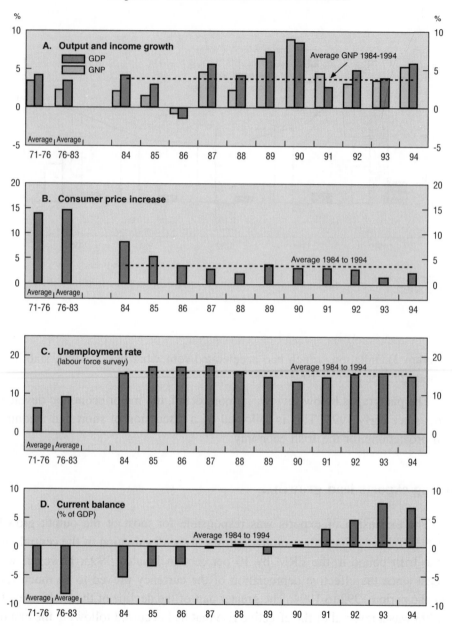

Source: Department of Finance and OECD.

Table 1. **Demand and output**

Annual percentage volume changes, 1985 prices

	1991 current price Irf million	1991	1992	1993	1994[1]
Private consumption	16 607	2.6	2.9	1.2	5.0
Public consumption	4 480	2.7	2.4	1.1	2.5
Gross fixed investment	4 642	−8.2	−1.9	−0.5	7.2
of which:					
Building and construction		0.6	0.6	−3.4	7.2
Machinery and equipment		−17.1	−4.8	3.2	7.2
Final domestic demand	25 730	0.5	2.0	0.9	4.9
Stockbuilding	639	−0.3	−2.8	−0.5	−1.2
Total domestic demand	26 369	0.1	−1.2	0.2	3.5
Exports	16 893	5.2	13.2	9.6	10.5
Imports	15 072	1.3	5.4	5.9	8.5
Foreign balance[2]	1 821	2.8	6.1	3.8	3.1
GDP (market prices)	28 189	2.9	5.0	4.0	6.0
Net factor income	−2 865	−8.2	17.6	6.1	8.9
GNP[3]	25 324	4.6	3.3	3.6	5.5
Memorandum items:					
Household saving ratio (per cent)		10.7	11.8	14.2	13.0
GDP (factor cost)	25 313	1.3	4.0	4.1	..
of which:					
Agriculture	2 218	−1.0	8.5	−6.1	..
Industry	9 432	3.0	8.1	4.7	..
Distribution, transport and communication	4 859	0.0	−1.3	1.9	..
Public administration and defence	1 480	−0.9	2.4	1.7	..

1. OECD estimates.
2. Contribution to GDP growth.
3. Expenditure measure.
Source: CSO *National Income and Expenditure*; OECD Secretariat.

the end of 1993 and most of this fall was eliminated by the end of 1994. Still, the decline did give Ireland some gain in international competitiveness, despite a slightly more rapid increase in manufacturing wages compared to its trading partners in 1993 (Diagram 4). When measured in a common currency, Irish wages fell 4.4 per cent relative to the other OECD countries in 1993 – more than offsetting the increase that had occurred in 1992. Compared with the United Kingdom, though, Ireland's relative wage rose 1.4 per cent in 1993.

Diagram 4. **MEASURES OF COMPETITIVENESS**[1]

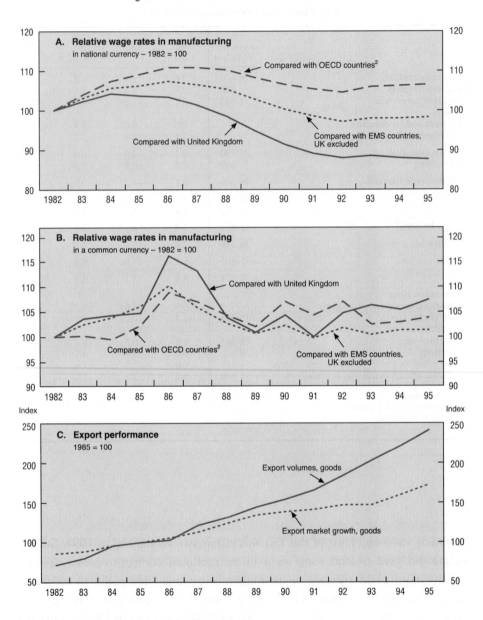

A. Relative wage rates in manufacturing
in national currency – 1982 = 100

Compared with OECD countries[2]

Compared with United Kingdom

Compared with EMS countries, UK excluded

B. Relative wage rates in manufacturing
in a common currency – 1982 = 100

Compared with United Kingdom

Compared with OECD countries[2]

Compared with EMS countries, UK excluded

Index

C. Export performance
1985 = 100

Export volumes, goods

Export market growth, goods

1. Relative to trade-weighted average of trading partners.
2. Mexico and Turkey excluded.
Source: OECD.

10

Comparisons of unit labour costs in a common currency show much larger gains in Irish export competitiveness. This indicator, however, is not an accurate measure in the case of Ireland due to the pace of structural change in its manufacturing sector, where a small number of industries with high productivity are growing in importance (see Box). In 1994, in contrast, Ireland experienced a small loss in competitiveness as a result of the appreciation of the currency, reducing the decline in Ireland's wages relative to the OECD countries generally since 1991 to only 1.2 per cent.

The small gain in competitiveness in 1993 helped sustain sales abroad from the traditional manufacturing sector in the face of negative growth in its export markets in 1993. The decline in Irish export markets, though, was relatively small compared to that experienced by other European countries as a result of the United Kingdom's early economic recovery. Indeed, the United Kingdom accounts for over a quarter of Ireland's total exports and is an especially important market for the traditional sector. Moreover, Irish producers gained competitiveness in the UK market relative to third-country exporters in 1993. These factors helped keep manufactured exports by the traditional sector basically unchanged in 1993, following a 9 per cent increase the preceding year (Table 2).[1] Agricultural exports also declined in 1993, in contrast to the 28 per cent rise the previous year.

Almost all of the 10 per cent growth in total exports in 1993 came from the "high-tech" sector. This sector was aided by its links to the more buoyant US market. The depreciation of the pound, however, appeared to have little impact on high-tech exports since the share of Irish costs in the total value of production is small. The decline in the currency, though, did lead to a rise in the pound price of such exports of about 6½ per cent in 1993 since high-tech Irish companies price their output at world prices. The rapid growth of high-tech exports may have been linked instead to increases in production capacity, particularly in the case of office machinery (mainly personal computers), where export volume in 1993 increased by 36 per cent. The increase in the value of high-tech exports amounted to about 9 per cent of GNP in 1993. Its impact on growth, however, was much less, due to a 18 per cent rise in repatriation of profits and royalties in that year.[2]

Import volume growth accelerated to 6.6 per cent in 1993, as increased production of high-tech goods required growing imports of inputs.[3] The rise in

Table 2. **Exports and imports of goods**

	1989	1990	1991	1992	1993[1]	1994[2]
A. Volumes and prices (per cent change)						
Total exports	11.2	8.5	5.5	13.8	10.0	12.6
Agricultural	5.6	–8.7	6.6	28.3	–12.3	0.8
Industrial	12.9	11.8	5.8	11.4	13.7	12.5
High technology	15.3	10.8	4.2	13.1	25.7	16.3
Traditional	10.1	13.0	7.8	9.4	–0.8	6.6
Total imports	13.0	6.9	0.7	4.8	6.6	9.1
Capital goods	27.6	4.3	–9.9	–3.3	30.9	9.0
Consumer goods	8.1	11.9	4.4	4.1	–3.4	7.0
Materials	12.0	5.7	1.5	7.1	5.1	10.0
Export prices	6.7	–9.5	–0.7	–2.7	7.6	2.1
Import prices	6.5	–5.0	2.3	–2.1	5.2	4.1
Terms of trade	0.2	–4.7	–3.0	–0.6	2.3	–1.8
B. Percentage share in total export volume						
Agricultural (including forestry and fishing)	17.2	15.0	15.0	17.1	13.6	n.a.
Industrial	81.1	83.1	83.8	82.1	80.5	n.a.
of which:						
High technology	45.0	45.6	45.6	45.4	49.2	n.a.
Traditional	36.1	37.6	38.2	36.7	31.2	n.a.
Percentage of exports to the United Kingdom	33.5	33.7	32.0	31.5	28.5	n.a.

n.a. = not available.
1. Sectoral level comparisons between 1992 and 1993 should be treated with particular caution because the introduction of Intrastat in 1993 led to large unclassified (by commodity) balances for both import and export statistics. The 1993 volume growth rates in this table reflect the allocation of these balances to sectors on a pro rata basis (pro rata to the shares of those sectors in total imports and exports).
2. First eight months of 1994.
Source: Department of Enterprise and Employment.

import volumes, though, still lagged behind that of exports, helping boost the merchandise trade surplus to Ir£ 4.8 billion in 1993, equivalent to almost 17 per cent of GNP (Table 3). Price factors also contributed to the expansion of the trade surplus: a 7.6 per cent rise in export prices, the first since 1989, coupled with falling prices for oil and other commodities resulted in a substantial improvement in Ireland's terms of trade.[4] The higher merchandise trade surplus was only partially offset by a larger invisible deficit in 1993, despite the increase in outflows of profits and royalties. The rise in the tourism surplus from 1.6 per cent of GNP to 1.9 per cent in 1993 and a small decline in gross payments on foreign private borrowing limited the increase in the invisible deficit. Current transfers

Table 3. **The current account of the balance of payments** [1]

Ir£ million

	1989	1990	1991	1992	1993	1994 [2]
Exports, f.o.b.	14 358	14 100	14 675	16 387	19 450	21 814
Imports, c.i.f.	12 114	12 286	12 688	13 020	14 621	16 549
Trade balance	2 244	1 814	1 987	3 367	4 829	5 265
Tourism, net [3]	286	430	519	432	531	650
Other services, net	–753	–642	–685	–811	–985	–1 057
Total services, net	–467	–213	–166	–378	–453	–407
Net factor income [4]	–3 233	–3 131	–2 865	–3 295	–3 804	–4 231
of which:						
Credits	1 345	1 639	1 762	1 643	1 626	1 700
Debits	4 578	4 770	4 627	4 938	5 430	5 800
Profits repatriation, etc.	2 564	2 507	2 377	2 888	3 426	3 900
Government debt interest	973	1 009	1 031	923	1 021	1 041
Other debt interest [5]	1 041	1 254	1 220	1 126	983	990
Current transfers, net	1 108	1 567	1 969	1 737	1 890	1 817
of which: EU [6]	1 051	1 450	1 842	1 632	1 773	1 519
Balance on current account	–348	37	925	1 431	2 462	2 445
Memorandum items:						
Per cent of GNP:						
Trade balance	10.1	7.6	7.8	12.6	16.9	17.0
Invisible balance	–11.7	–7.4	–4.2	–7.3	–8.3	–9.1
Current account balance	–1.6	0.2	3.7	5.4	8.7	7.9

1. National accounts definitions.
2. Secretariat estimates.
3. Including passenger fare receipts
4. Includes remuneration of employees.
5. Including semi-state bodies and banks' interest flows.
6. Excludes certain receipts arising from Ireland's participation in the European Monetary System.
Source: CSO, *Balance of International Payments,* and *National Income and Expenditure*, OECD Secretariat.

from the EU in 1993 remained near the previous year's level of about 6 per cent of GNP, while government debt interest payments abroad were also stable at about 3½ per cent. As a result, net fiscally-related transfers abroad remained near 2½ per cent of GNP.[5] With the increase in the merchandise trade surplus exceeding the rise in the invisible deficit, the current-account surplus rose to almost Ir£ 2.5 billion in 1993 or 8.7 per cent of GNP.

During the first half of 1994, export volume growth accelerated to 13 per cent over the first half of 1993. The gap in export growth between the modern and traditional sectors was much reduced. Import growth, meanwhile, picked up to 10 per cent. These volume changes more than offset some deterioration in the terms of trade, resulting in a further increase in Ireland's trade surplus to an estimated 17 per cent of GNP in 1994. This increase in the merchandise trade balance, though, was relatively small compared with the period 1991 to 1993, when it more than doubled from 8 to 17 per cent of GNP. Moreover, the surplus on trade in goods was expected to have been partially offset by a larger deficit on invisibles, as profit repatriation continued to rise in line with export earnings, and transfers from the EU declined. Consequently, the current-account surplus is estimated to have recorded a small rise in nominal terms, while falling as a share of GNP for the first time since 1989. The foreign balance, which had accounted for all but 0.2 percentage points of the 3.6 per cent rise in GNP in 1993, made a much smaller contribution to growth in 1994.

Followed by the recovery of domestic demand

Developments in exchange rate and monetary policy were major factors underlying the evolution of private domestic demand during 1993 and 1994. The environment of exchange rate and interest rate uncertainty and volatility in the first half of 1993 led households to increase their saving rate to 14.2 per cent for the year, the highest rate in more than a decade. Consequently, personal consumption increased only 1.2 per cent in 1993 (Table 1), despite a 4 per cent rise in real personal disposable income. However, growing consumer confidence led by a fall in interest rates and continued employment growth helped to generate a recovery in the second half of the year. The upturn continued into 1994, reflected in strong retail sales and new car registrations (Table 4), as declines in interest rates further boosted consumer confidence and reduced the household saving rate. A marked reduction in income taxation in 1994 helped sustain disposable income growth. With the decline in the saving rate, personal consumption outlays increased by an estimated 5 per cent.

Business fixed investment decreased for the third consecutive year in 1993 despite a rise in the profit share (Diagram 5). The fall reflected the impact of high interest rates and uncertainty amongst domestic companies about their prospects, in light of the slowdown in many of Ireland's major trading partners. The decline occurred despite a rise in investment in machinery and equipment that reflected

Table 4. **Recent economic indicators**

Percentage changes from a year earlier

	1991	1992	1993	1994	1994			
					Q1	Q2	Q3	Q4
Manufacturing output	3.2	10.2	5.4	..	7.3	12.0	13.3	..
Employment								
Manufacturing[1]	0.5	−0.3	−0.1	..	0.6	..	..	..
Building and construction[2]	−3.3	−2.0	−6.0	..	−1.1	2.3	4.6	..
Retail sales, volume								
Total	−0.1	2.3	1.4	..	9.3	5.7	3.8	..
New private car registrations	−17.8	−1.0	−5.3	25.1	45.7	19.2	8.1	−4.4
Dwellings completed[3]	−0.3	13.6	..	..	..	..	..	..
Exports, volume	5.6	13.7	10.2	..	13.7	12.3	..	..
Imports, volume	0.8	4.8	6.3	..	11.4	10.5	..	..
Trade surplus (Ir£ million)[4]	2 168	3 434	4 858	..	1 211	..	..	..
Total unemployment rate	14.7	15.5	15.8	14.8	15.2	14.8	14.7	14.6
Average weekly earnings[5]	4.4	4.0	5.4	..	..	..	..	..
Consumer price	3.2	3.0	1.5	2.4	1.7	2.7	2.5	2.4
Exchequer revenue	6.1	6.7	8.3	..	24.8	28.7	−7.0	..

1. CSO quarterly estimates of employment in industrial establishments with three or more persons engaged.
2. Building employment index for firms in private sector with five or more persons engaged.
3. Excluding local authority dwellings.
4. Quarterly figures are the total of seasonally-adjusted monthly data.
5. All industrial workers in manufacturing.
Source: CSO, *Economic Series.*

the strength of the modern sector. But the increase in this type of investment, which is generally supplied by imports, was more than offset by a fall in building and construction investment, which generates more domestic value added. In 1994 business investment is estimated to have risen more than 7 per cent in response to lower interest rates, a continued rise in profit share and the brighter outlook in overseas markets. Much of it appears to have been concentrated in the rapidly-expanding modern sector, which accounts for about 30 per cent of total manufacturing employment. The recovery in investment seems to have spread to the traditional sector as well, where output increased 5 per cent year-on-year in the first eleven months of 1994.

Housing investment fell about 4 per cent in 1993 as the high interest rates in the first part of the year discouraged residential construction. However, the fall in interest rates and the availability of cheap fixed-rate mortgages sparked a recov-

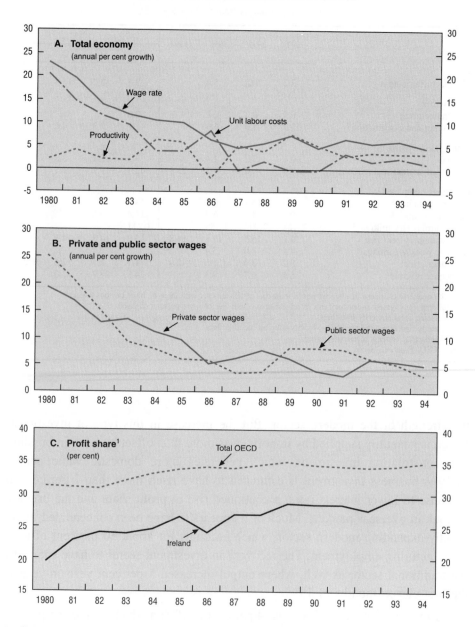

Diagram 5. **WAGE RATES AND PROFIT SHARE**

A. Total economy
(annual per cent growth)

Wage rate

Unit labour costs

Productivity

B. Private and public sector wages
(annual per cent growth)

Private sector wages

Public sector wages

C. Profit share[1]
(per cent)

Total OECD

Ireland

1.   Share of the non-wage component in net output of business sector.
Source: OECD.

16

ery in the latter part of the year, which continued into 1994. In the first three quarters of 1994, the number of dwellings completed increased 20 per cent over the year-earlier period, mainly in the private sector.

Government consumption increased by only 1 per cent in volume terms in 1993, though the real increase in public demand was larger, given the 5.2 per cent real rise in public service wages. In 1994, there was a slight acceleration in government consumption and also a large rise in the Public Capital Programme, which is partially supported by EU Structural and Cohesion Funds (see Part II). In addition, there was a continued rise in social welfare spending, which has helped boost total expenditure (excluding debt interest payments) from 36 per cent of GDP in 1990 to nearly 38 per cent in 1994. This is a reversal of the declining trend in the late 1980s, which had reduced spending from a peak of almost 44 per cent in 1986. One factor has been a substantial increase in spending on health and education as agreed in the central wage agreements, the 1991 to 1993 *Programme for Economic and Social Progress* (PESP) and the *Programme for Competitiveness and Work* (PCW), which took effect in 1994.

Inflation remains under control as unemployment falls

Overall wages increased almost 6 per cent in 1993 despite a depressed labour market (Diagram 5). In the manufacturing sector, hourly earnings rose by 5.3 per cent in the year to December 1993, considerably above the 3.75 per cent rise allowed under the central wage agreement. One reason for the large rise was the ''Local Bargaining Clause'' in the PESP, which permitted employers to grant additional pay increases subject to a limit of 3 per cent of basic pay over the three-year period. Much of the increase allowed by this clause occurred in 1993. Between 1990 and 1993, the agreement implied a 14.5 per cent maximum cumulative rise in wages except in the public sector where deferred payments were made and in industries covered by special clauses such as the construction sector.[6] In consequence, basic wages in those sectors increased by 24 per cent over the three years. However, even in the manufacturing sector, where there were few special clauses, wages rose by 16.6 per cent during the three-year period, reflecting ''wage drift'', which resulted from changes in working hours and shifts in employment grades. In 1994, the PCW, which limited the increase in basic wages to 2 per cent, came into effect. By the first quarter of 1994, the year-

17

on-year increase in manufacturing wages had slowed to 4½ per cent. With the deceleration of wage growth, the rate of increase of unit labour costs also slowed during 1994.

Despite the depreciation of the Irish pound, the rate of inflation (as measured by the consumer price index excluding mortgage interest payments) declined to 2 per cent in 1993. The inflationary impact of the fall in the exchange rate was offset by the stability of food and energy prices (Table 5). In addition, domestic manufacturers raised their prices for goods sold in the home market by much less than for goods that were exported. Depressed conditions in domestic markets and

Table 5. **Prices, wages and non-wage incomes**

Percentage changes over preceding period (annual rates)

	1989	1990	1991	1992	1993	1994
Consumer prices						
All items	4.0	3.4	3.2	3.0	1.5	2.4
All items except mortgage interest	3.9	3.4	3.2	2.8	2.0	3.0
Food	4.7	1.7	1.4	1.7	0.3	3.5
Energy	4.2	2.7	1.5	−1.7	0.3	0.3
Wholesale prices	5.6	−2.8	1.2	0.8	4.8	--
Manufacturing [1]	4.8	−1.6	0.8	1.7	4.6	1.1
Agriculture [2]	5.0	−11.3	−3.2	3.0	7.0	1.1
Deflators						
GDP	4.3	−1.7	1.1	1.3	3.6	--
Domestic demand	3.6	1.5	3.4	3.6	3.0	--
Exports of goods and services	7.3	−8.3	−0.4	−2.2	6.7	--
Imports of goods and services	6.9	−4.2	2.5	−1.1	4.8	--
Wages [3]	3.9	4.5	5.6	4.6	5.8	--
Non-wage incomes						
Non-agricultural sector [4]	13.9	3.8	6.4	6.0	16.7	--
Total business sector [5]	28.7	28.5	28.5	27.7	29.5	30.4
Memorandum item:						
Real wages [6]	−0.2	1.2	2.3	1.4	4.3	--
Terms of trade	0.2	−4.7	−3.0	−0.6	2.3	--

1. Price index of manufacturing industry output.
2. Price index of total agricultural output.
3. Hourly earnings in manufacturing.
4. Trading profits and other professional earnings in the non-agricultural sector.
5. Share of the non-wage component in net output of the business sector, OECD calculations.
6. Hourly earnings in manufacturing deflated by the consumer price index (all items).
Source: CSO, *Economic Series; National Income and Expenditure*, OECD Secretariat.

the delayed impact of the 1992 fall in import prices made it difficult for producers to increase prices. Inflation did accelerate during 1993, though, from the low 1 per cent year-on-year rate recorded in February in the wake of the temporary appreciation of the pound against sterling to 3.2 per cent by the end of the year. This pickup in inflation reflected improved conditions in domestic markets and the impact of higher import prices. In February 1994, inflation reached a peak of 3.5 per cent year-on-year as the effect of higher excise taxes was felt. Inflation, whether including or excluding mortgage interest payments, fell to about 2½ per cent in the fourth quarter of 1994 as a result of slower increases in unit labour costs. For the year as a whole, the rate of inflation for all items was 2.4 per cent, a rate on a par with the United Kingdom and Germany as well as the OECD average excluding Mexico and Turkey (Diagram 6).

There was a marked increase in employment as the economic expansion spread from the modern sector to the rest of the economy. Following a rise of 7 000 in 1993, the number of employed jumped by 30 000 in 1994, a gain of

Diagram 6. **CONSUMER PRICE INCREASES**

12 month change in the consumer price index

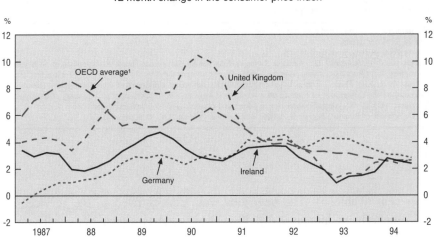

1. Excluding Mexico and Turkey.
Source: OECD, *Main Economic Indicators.*

Table 6. **Labour market developments**

	Memorandum item: Number (000s)	Annual percentage growth rates April each year					
	1994	1989	1990	1991	1992	1993	1994
Population							
Natural increase	18	0.6	0.5	0.6	0.6	0.6	0.5
Net immigration[1]	–10	–1.2	–0.7	–0.1	0.1	–0.2	–0.3
Total	3 571	–0.6	–0.1	0.6	0.7	0.4	0.2
Working-age population[2]	2 262	–0.2	0.6	1.4	1.4	1.2	1.1
Labour force[3]	1 397	–1.5	1.6	2.4	1.3	1.1	1.6
Total employment[3]	1 176	–0.2	4.2	0.0	0.4	0.6	2.6
of which:							
Manufacturing	231	4.8	2.7	0.0	0.4	–0.9	3.1
Building and construction	79	–4.3	13.4	2.6	–5.1	–4.1	11.3
Services	708	–1.3	4.0	2.0	1.8	3.3	2.6
Agriculture	140	–1.8	4.3	–8.3	–1.3	–5.9	–2.8
Manufacturing, by nationality[4]							
Irish		1.3	1.4	–1.7	–0.5	0.6	1.4
Foreign		4.7	4.2	–1.9	1.6	3.2	9.6
Public sector employment[5]		–4.3	–0.8	1.2	–0.7	0.5	0.8
Total unemployment rate, per cent		14.7	13.3	14.7	15.5	15.8	14.8
Memorandum items:							
Notified redundancies (000s)		13.4	13.3	16.7	18.2	18.2	15.8
Registered unemployed (000s)[6]		231.6	224.7	253.9	283.1	294.3	282.4
Labour force participation rate, per cent		61.0	60.3	60.9	61.5	61.5	61.8

1. Net immigration is calculated as a residual and expressed as percentage of the population of previous period.
2. The 15 to 64 age group.
3. Labour Force Survey, mid-April figures.
4. Figures based on *Industrial Development Authority Employment Survey* conducted in November of each year. Trend shown may differ from that evident from the *Labour Force Survey* as the IDA Survey is based on returns from employers, whereas the *Labour Force Survey* is based on respondent's subjective assessment of their employment status.
5. Estimated by the Department of Finance on a whole time equivalent basis. Data refer to 1 January of each year.
6. Excluding workers on systematic short-time working and persons aged 65 years and over.
Source: Department of Finance, *Economic Review and Outlook 1994* and OECD Secretariat.

2.6 per cent (Table 6). The new jobs were concentrated in the service sector, where employment increased by 40 000 over the two-year period. There were also significant gains in the manufacturing and building and construction sectors in 1994, offsetting the continued decline in agricultural employment. The improved labour market situation stopped the upward trend in the unemployment rate, which peaked at 15.9 per cent in the first quarter of 1993.[7] Unemployment continued to decline during 1994, falling to 14.6 per cent by the end of the year.

In addition to the progress in creating new jobs, the fall in unemployment was helped by government training programmes and other initiatives, such as the Back to Work Allowance Scheme. These programmes resulted in a net reduction of more than 9 000 from the unemployment rolls during the first nine months of 1994, almost half of the total decline recorded during that period. A pickup in net emigration in response to improved job prospects in the United Kingdom and elsewhere was another factor lowering unemployment. However, net emigration, which was estimated at 6 000 in 1993 and 10 000 in 1994, remained far below the level of 1988 and 1989, when it exceeded 40 000 per year.

The fall in unemployment occurred despite demographic factors which are pushing up the overall participation rate. Indeed, although the movement of the structure of the labour force towards younger age groups with high participation rates is more than doubling the natural rate of increase of the working population, youth unemployment rates have fallen relatively sharply since mid-1993. In addition to increased employment, the flow of young people into the labour market has been reduced by government employment schemes, rising emigration and higher participation rates in tertiary education. In the year to September 1994, the number of unemployed persons under the age of 25 fell by 7 per cent, double the rate of decline recorded for older people. Despite the reduction in total unemployment, the proportion of long-term unemployed has continued to increase and now accounts for almost half of the total.

A favourable short and medium-term outlook

Against the favourable background of an economic recovery in Europe, the Secretariat projects that Ireland's real GNP will expand by 5 per cent a year in 1995 and 4½ per cent in 1996 (Table 7). Growth is expected to be led by private domestic demand. With continued employment growth and low inflation ensuring real wage gains, consumption might continue growing at about 5 per cent in real terms, assuming a modest fall in the household saving rate. Inflation should rise slightly from 2½ per cent in 1995 to 3 per cent in 1996 as the unemployment rate declines further to below 14 per cent in 1996.

Table 7. **Short-term projections**

	Ir£ million (current prices)	Per cent changes		
	1993	1994	1995	1996
A. Demand and output (volume)				
Private consumption	18 065	5.0	5.1	4.7
Government consumption	5 167	2.5	2.5	0.0
Gross fixed investment	4 808	7.2	8.0	7.0
Final domestic demand	28 040	4.9	5.2	4.4
Stockbuilding [1]	−179	−1.2	−0.2	0.1
Total domestic demand	27 861	3.5	5.1	4.6
Exports	21 871	10.5	8.8	7.2
Imports	17 442	8.5	9.0	7.4
Foreign balance [1]	4 429	3.1	1.6	1.4
GDP at constant price	32 290	6.0	5.7	5.0
Net factor income [1]	−3 727	−0.5	−0.7	−0.5
GNP at constant price	28 563	5.5	5.0	4.5
B. Inflation				
GDP deflator		1.7	2.5	3.0
Private consumption deflator		2.4	2.6	3.0
Import deflator		4.2	1.9	2.1
C. Labour market				
Total employment (thousands)		2.6	2.4	1.9
Unemployment (rate)		14.8	13.9	13.6
		Per cent of GDP		
D. Current-account balance	7.6	6.9	6.7	6.2
E. General government financial balance	−2.3	−2.2	−2.5	−2.7

1. Contribution to GDP growth.
Source: OECD Secretariat.

These projections are based on the following assumptions:

- a constant effective exchange rate from March 1995 onwards based on a rate of 2.31 against the DM and 100p against sterling;
- a 9 per cent expansion of Ireland's export market for manufactures in 1995 followed by a 7½ per cent increase in 1996;
- an 8 per cent rise in the OECD oil import price in 1995 to $15.83 per barrel, remaining constant in real terms thereafter;
- a rise in short-term interest rates to 6.7 per cent in 1995 and 7 per cent in 1996 with the differential with German rates falling back to 80 basis

points in 1996. Long-term rates are projected to fall to 8¼ per cent in 1996, in line with the drop in the United Kingdom rates.

One possible risk to the economic outlook is an acceleration of inflation as the unemployment rate approaches the previous cyclical low recorded in 1990. This could cause local pay settlements to run ahead of the central wage agreement, possibly resulting in higher inflation and a loss of international competitiveness. If such developments are avoided, the economy would be firmly ensconced on a high-growth, low-inflation path that might well continue until the end of the decade. The OECD's medium-term reference scenario[8] has real GDP, which expanded at a 5.4 per cent annual rate between 1987 and 1994, growing at a 4½ per cent rate until the year 2000, while inflation, as measured by the GDP deflator, is projected to average less than 3 per cent. The major factors behind this favourable projection are Ireland's competitive strength and demographic factors. The economy's competitiveness leaves it well positioned to benefit from the projected recovery in Europe. Consequently, the foreign balance is projected to make a positive contribution to growth. The significant demographic changes that have occurred over the past 20 years should also have a favourable impact on per capita incomes. The dependency ratio will fall as the proportion of the population in the working-age group increases. The rapid growth of the labour force, though, will slow progress in reducing the unemployment rate, which is projected still to be as high as 13½ per cent in the year 2000.

II. Macroeconomic policies

For a number of years, economic policy in Ireland has been geared towards achieving a low and stable rate of inflation and reducing the size of government debt relative to national income. Considerable progress has been achieved on both grounds since the late 1980s. Inflation has averaged 2¾ per cent so far this decade, a level well below the post-war historical average. Public debt has been reduced from 116 to 90 per cent of GDP while government borrowing has remained low at around 2 per cent of output. Maintaining a stable exchange rate in the European Exchange Rate Mechanism (ERM) has been a key element of the macroeconomic strategy followed thus far. However, speculative attacks beginning in the autumn of 1992, which were associated with a sharp depreciation of sterling and very considerable turbulence in European exchange markets generally, ultimately forced the government to devalue the currency within ERM at the end of January 1993. Despite this, the depreciation of the Irish pound in trade-weighted terms was limited and was reversed in large part over the following year. As a result, past successes against inflation have not been jeopardised. Incomes policy – in the form of a centralised agreement between the government, unions, industry and farmers – played an important role in stabilising inflationary expectations in the labour market following the devaluation. At the same time, inflows of capital after the devaluation allowed interest rates to fall progressively, which contributed to a significant acceleration in economic activity. These developments have been accompanied by a further reduction in government borrowing and debt, despite factors pushing up government expenditure. The paragraphs below review the monetary and fiscal stance as well as the contribution of incomes policy since 1993.

Monetary policy

Exchange rate stabilises and interest rates decline following the devaluation

Monetary policy in 1993 and 1994 has aimed at maintaining a low inflation rate and a stable value of the currency within the ERM following the devaluation of January 1993, when the central rate for the Irish pound in the ERM was reduced by 10 per cent. This brought the exchange rate of the pound against UK sterling back towards its level prior to the exit of the British currency from the ERM in 1992 (Diagram 7). The devaluation came after a sustained defence of the Irish pound which involved sharp rises in interest rates and substantial intervention in foreign exchange markets, leading to a fall in reserves (net of borrowing) from Ir£ 3½ billion at the end of 1991 to Ir£ ½ billion a year later. In the aftermath of the realignment, the Central Bank lowered short-term interest rates quickly while initially keeping a large differential against German rates. As a result, the Bank was able to rebuild exchange reserves, redeeming swaps and repaying borrowing from the European Monetary Co-operation Fund.

The pound has essentially kept within its previous narrow band limits (±2¼ per cent) in the ERM, even though these limits were formally widened to 15 per cent in August 1993. Consequently, decisions on domestic short-term interest rates, which followed the trend in German official rates, continued to be highly influenced by exchange-rate considerations (Diagram 8). This policy was evident on two occasions in 1994. When the rate against the DM weakened in the spring of 1994, the Central Bank did not fully match the cuts in the German Lombard rate, thereby allowing the interest rate differential relative to Germany to widen for about two months, until the pound strengthened. In September 1994, when Irish rates rose on the prospect of higher UK rates and the pound started to appreciate once again, the Central Bank intervened in domestic money markets to reverse the pressure and the pound stabilised. By the end of 1994, short rates were at 6¼ per cent, only 80 basis points higher than German rates and lower than UK rates. These differentials were similar to those at the beginning of 1992, indicating a significant restoration of policy credibility at the short end of the market (Diagram 8). This increased credibility was also reflected in the effective exchange rate which, by the end of 1994, was only one per cent below its level prior to the turbulence in the foreign exchange market (Diagram 7). The depreci-

Diagram 7. **IRISH POUND EXCHANGE RATE BEHAVIOUR**

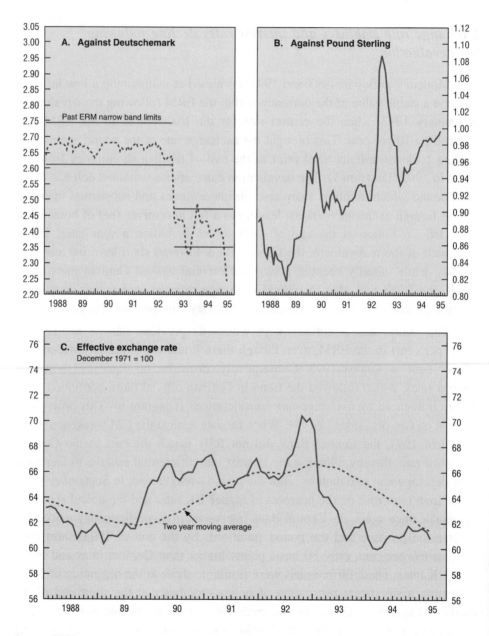

A. Against Deutschemark

Past ERM narrow band limits

B. Against Pound Sterling

C. Effective exchange rate
December 1971 = 100

Two year moving average

Source: OECD.

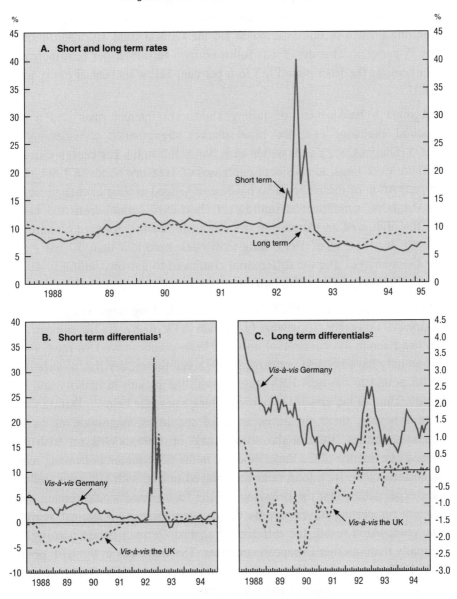

Diagram 8. **INTEREST RATE MOVEMENTS**

A. Short and long term rates

Short term

Long term

1988 89 90 91 92 93 94 95

B. Short term differentials[1]

Vis-à-vis Germany

Vis-à-vis the UK

1988 89 90 91 92 93 94

C. Long term differentials[2]

Vis-à-vis Germany

Vis-à-vis the UK

1988 89 90 91 92 93 94

1. Interbank rate for Ireland, FIBOR for Germany and Interbank loan for the United Kingdom.
2. 15 years central government bonds for Ireland, 7-15 years public sector bonds for Germany and 10 years government bonds for United Kingdom.
Source: OECD.

ation of the pound against the DM has been largely compensated by a gradual appreciation against sterling and a rise *vis-à-vis* the dollar. In March 1995, the accelerating growth of domestic credit led the Central Bank to raise the official rate by ½ per cent. This move was followed by a further ½ per cent increase, to 7¼ per cent, as the Irish pound fell to 5 per cent below its central parity against the ECU.

Against a background of falling short-term interest rates and a stable DM-pound exchange rate, the bond market strengthened considerably during 1993 (Diagram 8). Yields on ten-year bonds fell to 6¼ per cent, a thirty-year low. There were large non-resident purchases of Treasury bonds in 1993, though some proportion of these appear to have been hedged against exchange rate risk, given the large simultaneous outflow of short-term capital from the banking sector that indicated an increase in the size of the banks' forward commitments (Table 8). By the end of 1993, long-term rates were less than 70 basis points above German rates and the differential continued to narrow, falling to 40 basis points by February 1994 (Diagram 8).

As in many other OECD countries, Irish long-term rates rose from February 1994 onwards, somewhat faster than in Germany. By the summer, bond yields had risen to 8½ per cent, almost 150 basis points above DM rates. Foreign investors may have become concerned both about the greater risk of volatility of the Irish pound in the new ERM regime with the pickup in activity and credit demand adding to the upward pressure on long rates (see below). During the first half of the year, these pressures were of the same magnitude as in many European countries. But, in the second half of 1994, yields on Irish bonds stabilised as evidence of the undershooting in the government borrowing requirement became clear. Irish long rates then stayed in line with UK rates, reflecting market expectations that the behaviour of the Irish pound would remain closely dependent on sterling developments despite its appreciation against sterling in recent years. As a result, the differential against German bonds narrowed, but less rapidly than in other European countries. The weakness in the Irish pound in March 1995 led to a further rise in bond rates to nearly 9 per cent, with differentials widening against most European currencies.

The small difference between long-term interest rates in Ireland and the United Kingdom can be explained by the fact that the economic cycles in the two countries are currently in line with each other and further advanced compared to

Table 8. **Capital account of the balance of payments**

Irf£ million

	1992	1993	1994[1]	1993		1994	
				1st half	2nd half	1st half	2nd half
Current account							
1. Current account surplus	1431	2 462	2 150	1 273	1 188	915	1 235
Capital account							
2. Market flows	−4 274	429	−1 327	1 324	−895	−583	−744
of which:							
Irish-pound government bonds	−1 809	1 672	−421	1 325	347	25	−446
Net flows through credit institutions	−1 343	−843	222	−241	−602	223	−1
Licensed banks	−1 513	−1 051	..	324	−727	..	..
Other financial institutions	170	208	..	83	125	..	..
Borrowing of State-bodies	131	−141	..	13	−154	..	..
Private capital flows[2]	−1 549	−781	−1 128	37	−818	−831	−297
Residual flows	296	522	..	190	332	..	..
3. Non-market flows	1 642	−1 135	−925	−466	−669	−134	−791
of which:							
Government direct borrowing[3]	980	−78	−390	469	−547	395	−785
EMCF debtor position	716	−716	..	−716	..	0	0
Other official capital	−54	−341	−535	−219	−122	−529	−6
4. Valuation adjustment to reserves	58	409	−135	11	398	0	−135
5. Change in official external reserves (1 + 2 + 3 + 4)	−1 143	2 165	−237	2 142	22	198	−435
6. Level of reserves (end-period)	2 113	4 278	4 041	4 256	4 278	4 477	4 041

1. Estimate by the Central Bank of Ireland.
2. Includes residual flows for 1994.
3. This differs from Government foreign-currency borrowing in that it excludes foreign-currency borrowing from resident banks and through Section 69 bonds.
Source: Central Bank of Ireland.

those in continental Europe. Consequently, the need for monetary restraint is arising earlier in Ireland than in other ERM countries. With the growth of domestic credit moving well above that of the growth of nominal GNP (see below) and the tightening of labour market conditions, the extent of domestic inflationary pressures will have to be carefully considered when deciding on future interest rate movements. In this regard, the wider fluctuation bands in the ERM give the authorities more freedom to pursue their goal of price stability.

Credit expands as the recovery gathers momentum

Private sector credit growth continued to be weak in 1993,[9] reflecting low credit demand from most sectors of the economy due to higher profits and retained earnings as alternative sources of finance for firms. In addition, there was a reluctance to increase debt, given the experience at the beginning of the year when short-term interest rates were high and particularly volatile. By the end of 1993, loan demand had picked up, especially for fixed-rate house mortgages, which became attractive due to low long-term rates and a low premium for the floating-to-fixed rate swaps that banks used to match assets and liabilities. The year-on-year increase in the value of house mortgage finance was almost 10 per cent in February 1994 and nearly 14 per cent in August. Bank credit expansion accelerated during 1994 as economic growth spread to most sectors, reaching nearly 7 per cent in the year to August 1994 (Table 9). By the end of the year, the annual growth of lending from all credit institutions had reached 11 per cent,[10] reflecting the more rapid development of residential mortgage lending.

Table 9. **Sectoral distribution of credit growth to the private sector**

	1992	1993	1994	1992	1993	1994
	February 1992/93	February 1993/94	August 1993/94	February 1992/93	February 1993/94	August 1993/94
	Ir£ million			Percentage change		
Agriculture, forestry and fishing	−99.4	42.1	102.5	−7.1	3.2	8.1
Energy	55.3	−15.7	−39.0	51.5	−9.7	−24.3
Manufacturing	−92.5	−120.2	−19.9	−5.5	−7.5	−1.4
Building and construction	−5.4	−74.5	4.4	−1.3	−18.3	1.3
Distribution, garages, hotels	33.5	−38.3	124.4	1.9	−2.2	7.5
Transport	84.6	−105.2	−11.4	25.8	−25.5	−3.2
Post and telecommunications	−11.7	1.6	−2.2	−28.3	5.4	−6.5
Leasing, etc.	−293.1	78.3	125.3	−37.9	16.3	25.2
Other financial	1 034.3	608.9	726.9	98.0	29.1	30.5
of which:						
domestic currency	..	..	66.8	..	..	..
foreign currency	..	..	660.1	..	..	..
Business and other services	81.8	14.1	123.9	4.8	0.8	7.0
Personal	118.5	167.6	394.7	2.8	3.9	9.0
House mortgage	132.5	212.6	319.4	6.3	9.6	13.9
Other housing	−38.0	−12.8	−27.6	−16.6	−6.7	−14.4
Other	24.0	−32.2	102.9	1.3	−1.7	5.4
Total	896.8	575.0	1 529.6	6.6	4.0	10.7
Total (excluding other financial)	−137.5	−77.2	802.7	−1.1	−0.6	6.8

Source: Central Bank of Ireland.

Money growth stabilises

The unwinding of the exchange rate crisis during 1993 led to a marked acceleration in the growth of the money supply, due to the rebuilding of official reserves as a result of capital inflows (Table 10). The expansionary effect of the increase in reserves was partly offset by sales of government securities that were larger than the government deficit and by the reversal of very substantial central bank lending to credit institutions. Overall, the extended broad money supply (M3E), which includes building society deposits and postal savings accounts, grew by over 16 per cent in 1993. The narrower concept (M3) grew even faster, as, during the currency turbulence, some banks adjusted the interest rates on their deposits more quickly than did building societies. In 1994, the growth of the money supply (M3E) fell to 8 per cent, falling below the increase of credit

Table 10. **Money growth and its counterparts**

	1991	1992	1993	September 1994	1991	1992	1993	September 1994
	Ir£ million Changes from previous year				Percentage Changes from previous year			
Money aggregates								
Extended broad money supply (M3E)	845.2	2 172.6	3 380.6	1 928.5	4.8	11.7	16.3	8.1
of which: Building society deposits	497.2	709.3	474.6	480.7	12.9	16.3	9.4	9.0
Broad money supply (M3)	483.9	1 093.9	3 149.0	1 568.7	3.9	8.4	22.3	9.3
of which: Term deposit accounts	590.7	2 158.3	2 668.8	1 332.6	4.2	14.8	15.9	6.8
Narrow money supply (M1)	21.0	25.2	714.0	415.2	0.7	0.8	22.2	11.7
of which: Current accounts	−30.1	−2.3	573.4	316.4	−1.6	−0.1	30.7	14.3
Counterparts to the increase in M3E								
Domestic credit	678.6	3 019.1	249.4	3 139.1	3.1	13.4	1.0	12.7
Monetary financing of budget deficit [1]	193.8	1 250.1	−1 262.7	648.1	6.4	38.9	−28.3	21.7
Private sector credit	484.8	1 769.0	1 512.1	2 491.0	2.6	9.1	7.2	11.5
Short-term foreign liabilities [2]	166.6	−943.3	3 228.0	−1 210.6	−4.0	23.6	−65.3	118.3
Official reserves (net)	364.3	−2 659.2	3 681.1	76.2	12.6	−81.7	616.8	1.8

1. Lending from all credit institutions less government deposits with Central Bank.
2. Including other liabilities of all credit institutions.
Source: Central Bank of Ireland.

31

demand as foreign exchange reserves stabilised. The growth of narrow money (M1) was more rapid given that the fall in short-term interest rates lessened the attractiveness of term deposits.

Incomes policy

In order to minimise the transition costs of the move to a low inflation environment that was implied by the desire to keep the Irish pound stable in the ERM, the government has sought to influence the growth of wages through a series of incomes policies. The most recent, the *Programme for Competitiveness and Work* (PCW) – a three-year agreement among the social partners (government, employers, trade unions and farmers) – was signed in February 1994. This programme was designed to ensure employment growth by 2 per cent annually while reducing the public debt-to-GNP ratio to 95 per cent by 1996 at a minimum.[11] As in the previous agreements, the 1988-90 *Programme for National Recovery* and the 1991-93 *Programme for Economic and Social Progress* (PESP), the PCW includes a ceiling on wage increases based, specifically, on the expected price rise over the period of the agreement. Wage increases are limited to 2 per cent in 1994, 2½ per cent in 1995 and 3½ per cent in 1996. In the last two years of the agreement, there is a minimum increase of Ir£ 3.50 per week for full-time adult employees. The agreement took effect immediately except in the public sector and the construction industry, where wage increases were delayed by five months, thus extending the duration of the agreement to three and a half years. The PCW does not include a "Local Bargaining Clause" which, under the previous agreement, allowed employers to negotiate additional pay rises in exchange for productivity increases.

As a counterpart to continued wage moderation, the PCW commits the government to reduce the tax burden on workers with a view to reversing the long-run increase in the share of total revenue derived from taxes on earned income. During the period covered by the programme, it is agreed to concentrate tax relief on workers with low incomes while raising the income threshold at which the higher tax rate comes into effect. These measures would help reduce both marginal and average tax rates, which appear to be major factors in wage bargaining. On the expenditure side, the PCW commits the government to increased spending on welfare, health, education and housing. The exact amount of tax relief and spending increases, however, are not specified in the agreement but are intended to be consistent with the authorities' fiscal goals.

There have now been three successive multi-year incomes policies in Ireland, each including centralised agreements between the social partners designed to restrain the growth of wages. Such policies are an attempt to overcome the lack of flexibility in the labour market which minimises the wage response to long-term unemployment and results in the growth of earnings reflecting changes in unemployment rather than its level. In the context of the past two years, such policies have been effective in neutralising the impact of the 1993 devaluation on wage settlements. The growth of hourly earnings in manufacturing was limited to 5.8 per cent during 1993, decelerating to only 4.4 per cent by the first quarter of 1994. These policies have had a "cost", though. In particular, wage moderation has been linked to concessions on public expenditure including relatively large pay increases for public sector employees. In addition, the incomes policies may have introduced some rigidity in relative wage structures. At a time when the longer-term demand for unskilled labour is shrinking, this rigidity runs the risk of increasing unemployment among the low-skilled.

Fiscal policy

The 1993 Budget: progress towards consolidation

The 1993 central government deficit – measured by the Exchequer Borrowing Requirement (EBR) – fell to Ir£ 690 million (2.4 per cent of GNP), about $\frac{1}{2}$ per cent of GNP (Ir£ 80 million) lower than the initial target and $\frac{1}{4}$ per cent lower than the 1992 outturn (Table 11). The faster-than-predicted economic growth in 1993 helped boost tax revenues. Also, with interest rates declining rapidly during the year, expenditure on debt service fell. These two factors allowed the government to make unplanned expenditure of almost Ir£ 150 million at the end of the year, covering an equity issue to Aer Lingus and an early payment of public service pay arrears, without exceeding the deficit target. Such decisions, though, further boosted the share of government expenditure (excluding debt interest) in GNP, continuing the upward trend that started in 1990. On a general government basis, the level of the primary budget surplus,

Table 11. **Budgetary developments**

Ir£ million

	1992 Outturn	1993 Budget	1993 Outturn	1994 Budget	1994 Outturn (Estimate)	1995 Budget
Current budget						
Net expenditure [1]	9 806	10 483	10 519	11 115	11 188	11 852
Sinking funds	207	207	198	204	206	225
Interest payments	2 142	2 260	2 159	1 987	2 004	2 143
Other expenditure	7 457	8 016	8 162	8 924	8 978	9 484
Revenue	9 360	9 958	10 140	10 846	11 203	11 542
Income and wealth taxation		5 208	4 981	5 583	5 823	5 783
Indirect taxation		4 496	4 723	4 875	5 011	5 413
Other	450	473	436	388	368	346
Deficit (– surplus)	446	525	379	269	–15	310
Capital budget						
Expenditure	1 885	2 390	2 216	2 456	2 376	2 768
On-budget	877	1 075	1 150	1 225	1 232	1 363
Off-budget	1 008	1 315	1 066	1 231	1 144	1 133
Resources	1 618	2 149	1 950	1 922	1 689	2 268
Internal	329	445	461	391	369	349
EU funds	281	389	378	300	176	411
Off-budget revenue	860	1 016	894	1 009	1 049	1 213
Off-budget borrowing	148	299	172	222	95	192
Deficit	267	241	311	534	687	503
Exchequer Borrowing Requirement	713	766	690	803	672	813
Expenditure						
Net total	10 476	11 351	11 471	12 136	12 246	12 990
Net excluding interest	8 334	9 091	9 312	10 149	10 259	10 847
Gross excluding interest	10 707	11 554	11 846	12 768	12 878	13 623
Gross total	12 849	13 814	14 005	14 755	14 865	15 766
Memorandum items (as per cent of GNP)						
Net expenditure	39.2	42.6	40.2	40.9	39.5	38.7
Revenue	36.6	39.7	37.7	38.2	37.4	36.3
Exchequer Borrowing Requirement	2.7	2.9	2.4	2.7	2.2	2.4
Net expenditure excluding interest	31.2	34.1	32.6	34.2	33.1	32.3
Gross expenditure excluding interest	40.1	43.4	41.5	43.0	41.6	40.6
Gross expenditure	48.1	51.8	49.0	49.7	48.0	47.6

1. In the budget, expenditure is shown net of receipts of Pay Related Social Insurance (PSRI) contributions and offsetting revenues attributable to expenditure activities.
Source: Department of Finance.

Table 12. **Indicators of fiscal stance**

Percentage of GDP

	1990	1991	1992	1993	1994	1995
General government						
Financial balance	–2.2	–2.1	–2.2	–2.3	–2.2	–2.5
Primary balance	5.7	5.5	4.8	4.3	3.5	3.2
Domestic deficit	1.0	–0.2	–0.9	–0.6	–1.0	–1.2
Foreign deficit[1]	–3.2	–1.9	–1.4	–1.7	–1.3	–1.3
Structural balances[2]						
Financial balance	–3.4	–2.4	–2.5	–2.2	–2.2	–2.6
Primary balance	4.6	5.2	4.6	4.4	5.3	3.1

1. The foreign fiscal deficit equals interest payments on the national debt to non-residents plus EU contributions less receipts from the structural funds of the EU. The figure for 1994 is an estimate.
2. Structural balances measure the government financial balance at a normal level of capacity utilisation. The general government financial balance is measured in accrual terms. It is commonly used for international comparisons and includes the expenditure and receipts of all levels of governments. Borrowing is shown net of lending.

Source: National Accounts, Department of Finance and OECD calculations.

which excludes debt interest payments, dropped to 4¼ per cent of GDP, about 1½ per cent lower than its 1990 level (Table 12). As this fall was matched by a reduction in interest payments of a similar value, the overall deficit remained constant as a share of GNP. As a result, the *net* debt ratio stabilised despite the devaluation of the pound, which in itself raised the value of the foreign debt (essentially denominated in ERM currencies) by about 4½ per cent of GDP in 1993. The *gross* debt ratio rose, though, due to the fact that, as noted above, the government sold bonds substantially in excess of its funding requirements in order to profit from strong demand from foreign buyers.

The 1994 Budget: expenditure increases and tax cuts

Due to the non-recurrent nature of the last-minute expenditure authorised in the 1993 Budget, the high yield expected from the tax amnesty and the favourable impact of strong economic growth on tax receipts, the government started 1994 with a very favourable budgetary position. Even so, the 1994 Budget was based on a policy of allowing a slight widening in the EBR to Ir£ 803 million (2.7 per cent of the projected level of GNP) (Table 11). In the event, the budget envisaged discretionary tax and current expenditure measures amounting to Ir£ 509 million and a widening of the capital deficit by Ir£ 213 million, a total discretionary impulse of 2½ per cent of GNP. However, this measure exaggerates the impact of fiscal policy on the economy as almost half of the measures in the current account of the Budget represented the funding of previously incurred off-budget liabilities.[12] Of the remaining changes, most were on the tax side and were aimed at lowering the personal tax burden on low-income earners. There were some base-broadening measures and increases in indirect taxation to offset the cuts in income taxation and levies. On the expenditure side, social welfare benefits were increased and new community employment schemes announced (see the next chapter on progress in structural reform for a discussion of the tax and welfare changes). Overall, gross expenditure excluding debt interest was projected to rise faster than GNP once again – even excluding the one-off expenditures. While conventional indicators show only a slightly stimulatory fiscal stance in 1994, the buoyancy of corporate tax receipts has enabled a reduction the personal tax burden. This development has had a further stimulatory impact on the economy.

By the end of 1994, the budget situation turned out to be better than forecast. Due to the buoyant economy, the tax projection was surpassed by almost Ir£ 380 million mainly due to rapid growth of indirect taxes and corporate tax payments from multinational and financial enterprises. However, expenditure increased about ¾ per cent faster than expected in the Budget, bringing the rise in gross non-interest government expenditure to 20 per cent in the two years ending in 1994. Most of the increase in expenditure was due to the decision to fund another portion of the Post Office pension fund deficit. Moreover, there was a delay in receiving payments from the EU budget which, together with the decision to further accelerate the recapitalisation of Aer Lingus, implied a large overrun of the capital-account deficit. Together, these factors offset about Ir£ 220 million of the higher-than-expected tax revenues. As a result, the EBR is estimated to have stabilised at Ir£ 672 million (2¼ per cent of GNP), about Ir£ 130 million below the budget forecast. This allowed the gross debt-to-GDP ratio to fall by 6 points to 90 per cent at the end of 1994, down from a peak of 116 per cent in 1986.[13]

General government net borrowing has also remained low since 1993 at about 2¼ per cent of GDP (Table 12). This measure of the deficit mirrors changes in the EBR as other levels of government do not use credit to any great extent, relying on transfers and grants from central government to balance their own income and expenditure. Gaps may occur in the year-to-year movements of the EBR and general government net borrowing due to the different definitions of central government used in each concept[14] and to the fact that financial transactions are included in the EBR.

Budget plans for 1995 and beyond

The Irish central government budget for 1995 aims for a borrowing requirement of 2.4 per cent of GNP (Ir£ 813 million) which is somewhat higher than the outcome for 1994 (Table 11). The discretionary tax cuts and expenditure increases announced in the budget amount to Ir£ 360 million in 1995. These totals overstate the *ex ante* change in fiscal policy in that they are measured from a baseline which assumes that there is no change in the nominal value of both social welfare benefits and income allowances. Had these items been indexed to prices and earnings, respectively, they would have added almost Ir£ 220 million to the budget deficit in a full year (Table 13). On the other hand, the full-year cost of the changes made in the budget may raise borrowing to over Ir£ 600 million. Taking both of these factors into account, the impact of the budget on the deficit is closer to Ir£ 400 million (1.1 per cent of GNP). On a full-year basis, the budget implies a general government deficit of 3.0 per cent of GDP, before allowing for a possible under-estimate of tax revenues. In 1995, the projected borrowing requirement will add about 2 per cent to outstanding debt. Given that nominal income is expected to rise by over 8 per cent, the debt-to-GDP ratio should fall to 85 per cent in 1995 from 90 per cent in 1994.

The principal changes to tax and expenditure are all oriented towards improving work incentives at lower income levels. The universal child benefit has been raised, while the additional benefit for the unemployed was left unchanged. In addition, the government has chosen to concentrate reductions in income tax and social security contributions on the low-paid, so reducing replacement rates at low income levels. Finally, in another move to increase employment, the government has raised the threshold for the payment of the lower (9 per cent) rate of employers social security contributions. The budget also includes one measure to widen the tax base through limiting the tax-deductibility of certain income transfers, mainly to children in higher education. The impact of this on the deficit will be offset by a decision to stop charging fees

37

Table 13. **Summary of 1995 Budget changes**[1]

	Ir£ million		Per cent GNP	
	1995	Full year	1995	Full year[4]
Discretionary changes				
Spending measures[2]	201	294	0.6	0.9
Tax reductions	213	411	0.6	1.2
Tax increases	−54	−89	−0.2	−0.3
Total	360	616	1.1	1.8
Tax flow-back[3]	−74	−127	−0.2	−0.4
Live Register impact of Budget	−9	−15	0.0	0.0
Impact on net borrowing	277	474	0.8	1.4
Financing of discretionary changes				
Cash balances (rundown)	108	108	0.3	0.3
Borrowing	169	366	0.5	1.1
Impact on Exchequer Borrowing Requirement				
Borrowing on unchanged policies	644	644	1.9	1.9
Discretionary borrowing	169	366	0.5	1.1
Overall borrowing requirement	813	1 010	2.5	3.0

1. This table differs slightly from the official presentation in that the reported changes are judged against a baseline which assumes a continuation of the bank levy and the PSRI income tax allowance even though they require new legislation each year. In the official presentation of the budget, this renewal is shown as discretionary.
2. Includes Ir£ 60 million for Equal Treatment liability established by Court hearings.
3. Includes Ir£ 6 million PRSI buoyancy from tax/spending measures.
4. Most of the changes introduced in the 1995 Budget only come into effect part way through 1995. Thus the increase in expenditure shown for 1995 is less than that for a full year.
Source: Department of Finance.

for higher education. Against this, the tax base has been narrowed by allowing local government service charges and house rents to be paid from pre-tax income. In addition, the tax deductibility allowed for investment in certain new businesses has been increased.

Other discretionary changes add only 0.5 per cent to government expenditure, principally through the expansion of the community employment schemes for the unemployed and a provision to finance the initial consequences of a legal decision to equalise certain past welfare benefits paid to men and women. While the limited changes in expenditure should slow the growth of government spending in 1995, several factors suggest that the extent of the slowdown is somewhat overstated in the budget. *First,* treating the rundown of cash balances in 1995 as negative expenditure reduces spending growth by nearly 1 per cent. *Second,* one-off expenditure incurred in 1994 has been incorporated into the base for calculating the 1995 increase, thus making the spending increase permanent from 1995 onwards. *Third,* only one-quarter of the full-year expenditure on educational fees and child allowances will be incurred in 1995. Overall, given that the general government deficit seems likely to rise despite rapid economic growth, indicators of the fiscal stance show an increase in the structural component of the deficit to about 2¾ per cent of GDP in 1995. This suggests that the room for manœuvre in framing the 1996 Budget may be limited, given the commitment of the government to restrain the growth of expenditure next year to only 2 per cent higher than the rate of inflation.

Debt developments: achieving the Maastricht criteria

The medium-term fiscal strategy aims at meeting the Maastricht requirements for participating in the European Monetary Union, *i.e.* limiting the general government deficit to 3 per cent of GDP and reducing progressively the debt-to-GDP ratio to 60 per cent of GDP. With the deficit criterion being met in recent years, the debt ratio has been on a sharply declining trend. This has been achieved despite a decline in the primary budget surplus from 6 per cent of GDP in 1989 to a projected 4 per cent in 1995 (Table 12) and a marked expansion of non-interest government expenditure from 33 to 38 per cent of GDP in the same period, which was not matched by a similar increase in taxation.

The fact that the fall in the primary surplus has not posed a problem for debt reduction is because the size of the surplus necessary to stabilise the debt has also been falling. Indeed, since the average interest rate paid on the public debt has declined and the growth rate of GDP has accelerated, the gap between these two variables, which is the key determinant of the size of the deficit consistent with a stable debt burden, has been eliminated. The primary balance which ensures a stable debt ratio has fallen to zero and has even been slightly negative in some years (Diagram 9). However, a further decline in the primary balance required to stabilise the debt ratio seems unlikely in the medium term. The growth of economic activity is now at, or even above, the rate that is sustainable over the medium term (probably about 4½ per cent) and while real long-term interest rates are high, it is not certain that they will fall in the future. Moreover, the government is unlikely to allow a rise in inflation and even if price increases were to accelerate, nominal bond yields would probably follow.

Diagram 9. **PRIMARY BUDGET BALANCE**[1]

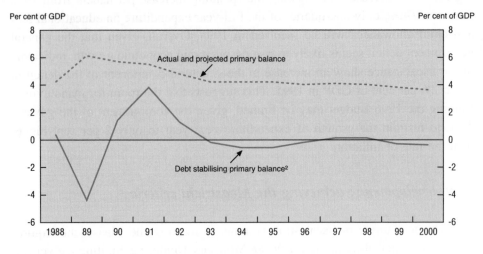

Per cent of GDP

Per cent of GDP

1. Actual balance minus interest payment on public debt.
2. The level of primary budget balance necessary to stabilise the ratio of government debt to GDP in a given year.
Source: OECD.

Achieving a further reduction in the debt ratio to meet the Maastricht criterion will require a marked slowdown in the growth of government expenditure such as that suggested in the policy programme of the new government. The Secretariat baseline medium-term projection of the Irish economy assumes that primary expenditure (*i.e.* excluding interest payments) grows in line with GDP from 1994 onwards (4½ per cent annually in real terms against an annual 8¼ per cent increase over the past five years). Such an increase in expenditure would reduce the debt ratio to 65 per cent by the year 2000, assuming that the share of taxes is held constant (Diagram 10). If primary expenditure were to continue to grow at the same pace as during the past five years, the debt ratio would remain broadly stable for a while before moving back towards 100 per cent of GDP. At the same time, the budget deficit would break through the 3 per cent limit in 1996 and quickly move up afterwards.

The new government has announced its intention to limit the *nominal* growth of expenditure to 6 per cent in 1995 and the *real* growth to 2 per cent annually thereafter. If this policy were adhered to for five years and if there were no reduction in the tax ratio, then the debt ratio would fall to 60 per cent by 1999,

Diagram 10. **ALTERNATIVE GOVERNMENT DEBT SCENARIOS**

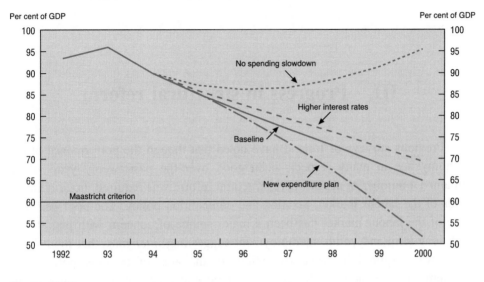

Per cent of GDP

Per cent of GDP

Source: OECD.

so keeping comfortably within the Maastricht criterion. Keeping expenditure growth under control in line with these objectives would mean that the EBR would be eliminated by 1997, with the budget then moving into surplus. Lowering debt in this way would create scope for a fall in long-term interest rates, as assumed in the Secretariat's baseline scenario. However, the behaviour of the debt ratio is becoming less sensitive to interest rate movements now that its level has come down. For example, if the average rate of interest on government debt were to increase by 1 per cent from 1995 onwards, the debt ratio would rise by at most 4 points by the end of the century and by less than that once allowance has been made for the significant proportion of interest payments that are fixed for ten or more years in advance.

III. Progress in structural reform

Previous surveys of Ireland have noted that though the performance of the economy has in many respects been good over the past twenty years, there remained a number of areas where structural reform was required, notably in the fields of the labour market, taxation and competition policy. The poor performance of the labour market has been a major source of concern with persistently high long-term and youth unemployment suggesting, *inter alia,* that more flexibility was required in wage formation. In the area of taxation policy, two problems were evident: high marginal tax rates at relatively low income levels and a low level of taxation on income from property. As for competition policy, concern had been expressed about the difficulty of starting procedures under the existing law. Since 1993, a number of initiatives have been taken by the government to address some of the problems identified above. Recent decisions at the level of the European Union will also have a significant impact on the Irish economy in the next few years. The GATT agreement should lead to a significant reshaping of the Irish economy moving it further away from an agricultural base towards industry. With respect to the financial system, Dublin and London stock exchanges will soon be separated and supervisory powers over the exchange will be given to the Central Bank. The present chapter looks at the measures introduced or planned in all of these areas.

Labour market

Ireland has an unusually high level of unemployment compared with other OECD countries. Almost half of the total unemployed have been without work for more than a year and have low levels of education. Government policy in recent years has aimed at increasing the incentives for the unemployed to work, though the measures have concentrated on those facing short, rather than long-term unemployment. In particular, the 1994 Budget introduced a significant number of changes to the benefit system, designed to reduce financial incentives to remain unemployed for short periods of time. Thus, the earnings-related supplement to unemployment benefits, which was payable for one year, was abolished. At the same time, unemployment benefits were made taxable, so lessening the extent to which newly-unemployed persons would be able to claim refunds of tax previously withheld from their salary. This measure only affects those who are employed and unemployed in the same year, as the unemployment benefit, by itself, is too low to result in a tax liability. The money thus saved was used to raise the flat-rate unemployment benefit by 9.7 per cent, bringing it to the same level as the means-tested unemployment assistance paid to the long-term unemployed. The net result of these changes is to reduce the average replacement rate (the ratio of income when unemployed to net income when employed) by about 6 to 7 percentage points from 42 to 35 per cent for a single person and from 70 to 64 per cent for a married person with two children.[15] Within these averages, the reduction is greatest for those whose in-work income was highest. The replacement rate was further reduced by the 1995 Budget, which cut taxes on the low paid, while keeping unemployment benefits in line with prices (see Part II).

While such reforms do contribute to improving the incentives to return to employment faced by the short-term unemployed, the real problem remains the level of long-term unemployment. In 1994, the benefits paid to the long-term unemployed were raised by more than the rate of inflation, though the gap, at about 0.5 per cent, was noticeably lower than in the past fifteen years when they have risen on average by 4 per cent per annum ahead of inflation in a context of stable real after-tax earnings for the average worker (Diagram 11). These trends have resulted in a continuous upward movement in replacement ratios for the long-term unemployed. While this ratio is still at a relatively low level of about 35 per cent for a single person with an earnings potential equal to the average wage, it rises as high as 75 per cent for a young person who has not successfully completed the junior secondary cycle of education[16] (Diagram 11), and even higher for other specific groups (see below).

Categories of the population with high replacement ratios tend to have high unemployment rates. An analysis of household income surveys showed that, in 1987, the unemployment rate of people with a replacement rate of less than

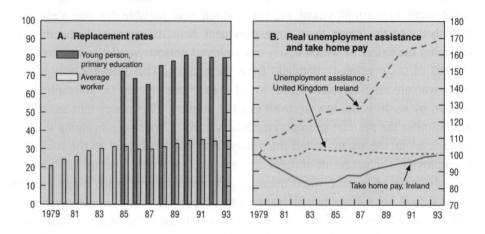

Diagram 11. **THE MOVEMENT OF EARNINGS AND UNEMPLOYMENT ASSISTANCE**

Single person

Source: Ministry of Finance and OECD.

40 per cent was 12 per cent, while the unemployment rate for those with a replacement rate of 80 per cent was over 50 per cent (Table 14). The concentration of high replacement rates amongst those with families was, in theory, improved by the introduction of the Family Income Supplement (FIS) in 1987, as it assures a minimum income for low-paid workers so increasing the gap between unemployment benefits and take-home pay. In practice, the take-up of this benefit may still be as low as one case in three, even though expenditure on this benefit has risen rapidly. Consequently, the FIS has had limited success in lowering replacement rates. Moreover, while it boosts the incentive to find a job, the FIS raises the disincentive to earn more once employed, since when an individual's wage increases, the supplement is progressively withdrawn. High replacement ratios amongst unemployed people with families occur because child benefits paid to the unemployed are (at Ir£ 17.40 per week in 1994) much higher than similar benefits paid to employees (Ir£ 4.60 per week), although this gap was narrowed by the 1995 Budget. A policy of equalising these grants at the higher rate and making them taxable would markedly strengthen work incentives,

Table 14. **Replacement and unemployment rates**

1987

	Replacement rate					
	0 to 20	20 to 40	40 to 60	60 to 80	80 to 100	over 100
	Per cent of labour force					
Unemployment rate	12.8	12.2	29.0	39.9	53.5	13.0
	Per cent of category with given replacement rate					
Total labour force	7.7	31.7	35.2	20.6	4.6	1.2
All unemployed						
Unemployed, single	6.2	24.9	55.6	12.9	0.2	0.2
Unemployed, married no children	0.0	6.3	59.5	23.5	10.7	0.0
Unemployed, married with children	0.7	1.0	13.0	60.4	23.6	1.2

Source: Callan, O'Donoghue, O'Niell (1994), "Analysis of basic income schemes for Ireland", ESRI Research paper 21, p. 55.

though there might be administrative difficulties in implementing it. Almost all of the replacement ratios over 100 per cent amongst the unemployed would be eliminated while the number of unemployed with a replacement rate over 80 per cent would be reduced by a factor of 10. The new government favours a gradual move in this direction. Full implementation of this policy would cost about Ir£ 240 million per year (3/4 per cent of GNP), allowing for the flow back of income tax.

Taxation

The 1994 Budget restarted the process of tax reform which had stalled in 1993 but changed the direction of the reform. Between 1985 and 1992, the focus had been on reducing the higher rates of marginal income taxation. The culmination of this process was the abolition of the top tax bracket, leaving just two rates. Including social security contributions paid by individuals, the highest marginal tax rate is now 56 per cent. These reforms, though, had little consequences for individuals with an average income. For a single person, the marginal tax rate has remained constant at just under 56 per cent (including the

Table 15. Income tax and social levies

Per cent of gross income, average earnings, single person

	Average earnings	Tax rates [1]		Proportion taxed [2] at:		
		Average	Marginal	Zero	Standard rate	Higher
1985	8 939	35.0	56.5	31.2	50.3	18.5
1986	9 606	34.2	55.5	31.1	48.9	20.0
1987	10 096	35.5	55.8	29.6	46.6	23.9
1988	10 575	34.5	55.8	29.7	53.9	16.4
1989	11 000	33.2	55.8	28.5	55.5	16.0
1990	11 424	32.3	55.8	27.5	56.9	15.7
1991	11 925	32.3	55.8	26.7	56.2	17.1
1992	12 405	30.8	55.8	25.7	60.3	14.1
1993	12 972	32.3	56.8	25.1	59.2	15.7
1994	13 556	30.9	55.8	25.3	60.5	14.2

1. Includes social security taxation and temporary income tax levies.
2. Income taxation only.
Source: Department of Finance and OECD.

employment, training and pay-related social insurance levies) while the average tax rate was reduced by just over 4 percentage points (Table 15). For such a person, the reduction of the lower income tax rate in the past decade, from 35 to 27 per cent, has mainly been offset by a reduction of the basic tax exemption relative to income levels. Moreover, for those at lower income levels, these changes have tended to increase the tax burden. In contrast, the 1994 Budget aimed to reduce the average tax rate of lower-paid workers while keeping standard marginal tax rates constant, though the temporary income tax levy of 1 per cent was also abolished.

The new policy, adopted in the 1994 Budget, of lowering the average tax rate for lower income levels was in part paid for by reducing the value of certain tax exemptions and by increasing property taxation. The overall cost of all such tax expenditures have been growing rapidly in the past decade with the loss in revenue rising from 8 to 18 per cent of total income tax revenue (Table 16). The 1994 Budget reduced two of the largest categories of tax expenditure, namely house mortgage interest and medical insurance premiums, by limiting relief to the standard rate of income tax. The change will be introduced gradually over a four-year and two-year period respectively and will raise, in total, Ir£ 80 million. A further broadening of the tax base was obtained by lowering

Table 16. **The cost of major special exemptions to personal income tax**

Ir£ million

	1980/81	1991/92
Pension fund income	30.0	216.0
Mortgage interest	36.0	181.0
Medical insurance	6.0	52.0
Government non-marketable debt	1.2	23.9
Government debt held abroad	16.0	113.0
Startup investment schemes	0.0	49.0
Total income tax foregone	89.2	634.9
Income tax yield	1 032.0	3 471.0
Per cent loss in tax	8.6	18.3
Memorandum item:		
Pension contributions	20.0	84.9

Source: Statistical Reports of the Revenue Commissioners.

both the valuation and income thresholds for the payment of the residential property tax. This tax is payable by households with an income of over Ir£ 29 500 owning residential property in Ireland, or abroad, with a total value over Ir£ 94 000. The excess of the value of property over this threshold is taxed at 1.5 per cent, a relatively high rate by international standards. The changes yielded a revenue of Ir£ 4 million.

The three largest remaining unrestricted domestic tax expenditures applying to income tax are the failure to tax the investment income of pension funds, tax relief on private pension contributions and the relief given to favour investment in certain small companies. The tax treatment accorded to private occupational pension schemes is a complex issue in which account has to be taken of the tax position on contributions to the schemes, the tax payments on the income of the scheme investments and the eventual tax treatment of money withdrawn from the schemes. The ability to pay contributions to a pension scheme from pre-tax income gives rise to an initial government subsidy compared to other forms of saving. However, if the pension paid by the scheme is fully taxed, the government eventually recuperates its initial subsidy. Only to the extent that a capital sum can be withdrawn from the scheme without payment of income tax, does the government not recover its initial subsidy. As, in Ireland, pension payments are fully taxed, the tax relief on contributions should not be regarded as tax expenditure. On the other hand, the failure to tax the income of occupational pension funds does generate a subsidy. It means that a higher rate of return can be earned by accumulating income within a pension fund than within other collective investment vehicles such as life insurance company funds or mutual investment funds which do not have this ability to shelter income from taxation.[17]

Schemes to favour investment in certain small businesses (the Business Expansion Scheme) have been the most rapidly growing component of total tax expenditures over the past decade. These schemes allow participants in approved projects to fully offset the cost of their investment against their highest marginal tax rate. Companies which meet the criteria for inclusion in a scheme thus receive, in general, a subsidy equal to 48 per cent of the initial investment, up to a ceiling of Ir£ 1 million. Such a subsidy could only be justified if there were evidence that the capital market in Ireland had severe imperfections. Experience in other countries suggests that such schemes rapidly become seen as tax shelters rather than fulfilling their original objectives.

Foreign trade

The structure of the Irish economy will be considerably affected by the GATT agreement reached at the end of the Uruguay Round in December 1993. This agreement resulted in a 37 per cent fall in the common external tariff of the EU. The fall in tariffs will be somewhat greater for imports from the United States and Canada but less for imports from Japan because of compositional factors. The overall impact on Irish industry is expected to be positive; one study[18] estimates that it will raise gross output by 3 per cent, mainly due to the overall buoyancy of world trade (Table 17). The effect on output, however, is likely to be negative for some industries, such as clothing, textiles and footwear. These industries will lose a significant degree of protection, both because of the progressive integration of the Multi-Fibre Agreement into the GATT framework with bound tariffs rather than negotiated quotas, and because imports from outside the EU will be able to be freely traded within the Union. (Previously there were individual quotas for each country and the Irish share of the total quota was especially low.) There is, however, a ten-year adjustment period and most of the change in tariffs comes at the end of that period.

Table 17. **Estimated impact of the GATT agreement on Irish manufacturing industry**

	Size of industry share in:		Increase in output and employment
	Output	Employment	
Office and data processing	10.1	3.7	7.5
Miscellaneous	4.8	6.4	6.5
Mechanical engineering	2.4	4.2	6.1
Chemicals	11.8	6.7	5.7
Electrical engineering	9.3	11.0	4.8
Instruments	2.7	3.9	3.7
Leather	0.3	0.2	2.2
Drink and tobacco	4.4	3.0	2.0
Ores and metals	4.2	7.1	1.6
Vehicles	1.8	3.2	1.4
Wood and furniture	1.9	3.8	1.3
Mineral products	6.9	9.6	1.1
Textiles	2.4	5.3	0.7
Food	31.3	18.3	0.6
Paper	4.0	7.2	0.2
Clothing	1.6	6.0	−4.3
Footwear	0.1	0.4	−4.8
Total gain in output			2.9
Total gain in employment			2.3

Source: Fitzpatrick Associates and A. Matthews (1993), ''The impact of the Uruguay Round on the Irish economy'', a report to the Ministry of Tourism and Trade.

Although there may be a gain on the industrial side, this will not be the case for agriculture. Indeed, the GATT agreement foresees a 36 per cent reduction in agricultural subsidies by 2000 compared with the average level of subsidies in 1986-90; internal support is to be reduced by 20 per cent, though some subsidies that do not vary with production are exempt; also there will be tariff quotas allowing a certain degree of access to the market for some products; and, perhaps most fundamentally, the variable levy on agricultural imports will be replaced by a fixed, bound tariff that will be reduced by 36 per cent over six years, thereby limiting the possibility of isolating EU prices from world prices. As the base for these changes is the level of subsidisation in 1986, they will include the impact of the 1992 CAP reforms. This reform is estimated to have already reduced output by about 2 per cent in 1995, with a 17 per cent fall in prices (Table 18), although the impact on farm income should be offset by a doubling of the value of subsidies. The remaining changes from the reform of the CAP and implementation of the GATT agreement that come into effect

Table 18. **Impact of CAP reform and the GATT agreement on agriculture**

	CAP reform			Uruguay Round		
	Volume	Value	Price	Volume	Value	Price
Beef	−2		−17	−5		−5
Dairy	−1		−2	−2		−5
Sheepmeat	−4		−15	−2		−5
Pigmeat	5		−10	−2		−5
Poultry	5		−10	−3		−5
Cereals	−8		−29	−5		0
Feed inputs	0		−17	−3		0
Output (market prices)		−14			−9	
Subsidies		108			−2	
Output (factor prices)		5			−7	

Source: Fitzpatrick Associates and A. Matthews (1993), "The impact of the Uruguay Round on the Irish economy", a report to the Ministry of Tourism and Trade.

after 1995 may reduce agricultural output by some further 3 per cent, leading to a fall in agricultural employment of about 4 000 people and an expected fall of about 7 per cent in agricultural incomes.

Overall, the net impact of the gain in employment in the industrial area is estimated to be greater than the loss in the agricultural sector, even without allowing for the unquantifiable, but presumably positive, impact of the GATT agreement on trade in services. Most of the gains in the industrial sector come through general trade buoyancy, because the agreement does not improve the already tariff-free trade with Europe but starts to unwind some of the trade diversion effects of the existing free trade in Europe.

Competition policy

The 1991 Competition Act reshaped Irish policy in this area by extending the principles of EU competition law to the domestic economy, which made anti-competitive practices illegal. The Act replaced the Fair Trade Commission with the Competition Authority, whose major task has been to consider requests from firms for exemptions from the Act for certain agreements and concerted practices.[19] By the end of February 1995, the Authority had dealt with 810 of the

1 277 agreements notified to it. As a result, 467 cases were outstanding, the bulk of which were filed after the law came into force. The large number of outstanding cases reflects the relatively small size of the Authority which had a staff of only twelve until it received additional resources in 1995. The Authority has treated cases that have common features first. As a result, it has designed standard agreements in two categories: exclusive distribution contracts (in petrol and other retail areas) and shopping centre leases, which have entailed the modification of some existing contracts. However, most of the cases where the notified exclusive distribution agreement includes restraints on competition (such as limits on freedom to set prices, or territorial protection, or limits on post-termination competition and the freedom to choose customers) have not yet been considered. Furthermore, the Authority lacks the power to begin investigations independently. Since the most egregious practices are unlikely to have been notified to the Authority for approval, it may, therefore, be unaware of the most serious violations of the Act. Finally, it appears that the decisions taken by the Authority are not always respected.[20]

In addition to its inability to implement its decisions regarding notifications, the Authority also lacks the power to enforce the provisions of the Competition Act. Enforcement relies primarily on private actions by "aggrieved person(s)". The possibility of obtaining damages, including exemplary ones, is intended to encourage injured parties to take legal action to eliminate abuses. The Minister for Enterprise and Employment can also initiate Court action, though not for damages. So far, however, there have been very few private actions under the Act and no ministerial actions. In 1994 the government introduced amendments to the 1991 Act to improve the enforcement of competition policy. The amended law would allow the Authority to initiate investigations and to take court actions either on its own initiative or as a result of third party complaints, but it still does not specify the fines or penalties for non-compliance. Moreover, the amended Act will lessen the responsibility of the Authority for deciding on whether or not mergers and take-overs are anti-competitive. In 1993, the Minister for Enterprise and Employment decided to double the thresholds for Ministerial consideration of mergers under the 1978 Mergers Act. It now applies to every proposed merger where the value of the gross assets of each of two or more of the enterprises involved is more than Ir£ 10 million or where the turnover of both firms exceeds Ir£ 20 million.

Financial markets

The government has introduced a bill for the regulation of stock-broking activities, making the Central Bank the supervisor of the Irish Stock Exchange. The law replaces a situation where there was only limited national regulation of the stock market. The only existing national legislation, dating from 1799, gave the government power to licence brokers in government stock. Since 1973, the Irish Stock Exchange has been in fact a unit of the International (London) Stock Exchange. Under the new law, the Central Bank will authorise all firms wishing to trade on any stock exchange in the country. Day-to-day supervision of the market will be undertaken by the exchange itself. The proposed legislation conforms to the relevant EU directives and so Irish brokers will be able to establish anywhere in the EU without further authorisation.

The National Treasury Management Agency has proposed a major reform of the government bond market, which currently functions on a dual capacity broker basis. The Agency favours the introduction of a market-making system with the aim of increasing liquidity. Primary dealers in a market-making system would be committed to continuous quoting of bid and offer prices on benchmark stocks, so that the immediacy of the market would be improved with instantaneous order-matching. The Agency is currently consulting market participants before submitting a formal proposal to the Minister of Finance for approval.

Summary

The principal structural problem facing Ireland remains the level of long-term unemployment. The reforms introduced in the 1994 Budget represent a continuation of the process of introducing more flexibility into the labour market. Further changes will be necessary for employers to offer low-paid jobs suited to the weak qualifications of many of the unemployed and to increase the incentives for the long-term unemployed to work. The gap between benefits and earnings is particularly small for inexperienced young people and those with families. Consideration should be given to paying the full rate of benefits only to those with substantial labour force experience, and to equalising the child benefits of those in employment with those of the unemployed. Reductions in taxation at lower income levels could also help to improve incentives and the necessary changes could be achieved through a continued broadening of the tax base. The Competition Authority, created in 1991, is now enjoying wider powers to contest anti-competitive behaviour more actively. The recent increase in the Authority's resources will help it make more effective use of these powers.

IV.   Education and training

Although Ireland has been one of the fastest growing economies in the OECD area over the past two decades, its income levels remain significantly below those in the richest countries (Table 19). Real output per person employed, after correction for differences in international price levels, has moved from 61 per cent of the OECD average in 1970 to an estimated 85 per cent in 1995. Given the high proportion of dependants in the population, real output per capita is even lower relative to the OECD average, at just under 70 per cent. In addition, despite rapid economic growth and relatively rapid job creation, the level of unemployment in Ireland is still one of the highest among OECD countries. The poor labour market performance affects primarily the young, who represent 42 per cent of the population and constitute a large proportion of the long-term unemployed (Diagram 12). In these circumstances, the challenge for the Irish authorities is to create the conditions for sustained growth in the years to come, in order to catch up with the level of incomes seen elsewhere in Europe, and to ensure that such growth is reflected in increased employment opportunities, so allowing a permanent reduction in unemployment.

Education and training policies will have a crucial role in this respect. Investment in education is as effective a form of capital accumulation as increases in physical capital. With rapid technical change altering the demand for skills and adaptability becoming a sought-after attribute, the benefits of education have tended to increase in recent years. The demand for high-level skills has risen in Ireland where poorly-qualified school leavers quickly become unemployed. While increased labour-market flexibility would help reduce this category of unemployment, it would not remove the problem of the falling demand and hence poor wages attached to low-skilled jobs. The perceived failure of the educational system to equip lower-ability school-leavers with qualifications that would allow them to participate in economic growth, rather than becoming

Table 19. GNP per worker and per capita[1]

1990 constant prices and purchasing power parities
OECD = 100

	1960	1970	1980	1985	1990	1995	2000
Per worker							
Ireland	**60**	**61**	**69**	**72**	**79**	**85**	**90**
Peripheral European countries[2]	77	82	88	88	89	92	93
Central European countries[3]	94	99	105	105	107	106	108
North American countries[4]	177	147	127	123	118	116	113
Pacific countries[5]	49	70	80	84	89	87	90
Other countries[6]	25	28	30	33	37	40	44
Memorandum item:							
European Union	84	89	96	97	98	100	101
Per person							
Ireland	**53**	**53**	**55**	**52**	**57**	**68**	**75**
Peripheral European countries[2]	78	80	81	80	82	81	83
Central European countries[3]	101	102	105	103	103	102	104
North American countries[4]	153	137	131	130	126	127	121
Pacific countries[5]	55	82	89	95	100	102	107
Other countries[6]	27	25	25	26	27	26	28
Memorandum item:							
European Union	87	88	91	89	91	90	93

1. Gross National Product has been used as the measure of total income.
2. Italy, United Kingdom, Spain, Portugal, Greece, Ireland, Iceland, Norway, Sweden, Finland, Denmark.
3. Germany, France, Netherlands, Belgium, Luxembourg, Austria and Switzerland.
4. United States and Canada.
5. Japan, Australia, New Zealand.
6. Mexico and Turkey.
Source: OECD.

unemployed, has led the Irish authorities to make a number of proposals for reforming the system.

The reforms envisaged cover a wide range of areas including the relationship between the owners of schools (often still the church) and the community; the governance of schools; the role of the Department of Education; and most importantly, policies to assist the performance of low-performing primary and secondary schools in order to reduce the number of children who leave school without basic skills.[21] The reform process started with a consultative document issued by the government in 1992, followed by a national convention open to all

Diagram 12. **LONG-TERM UNEMPLOYMENT RATE**
1992

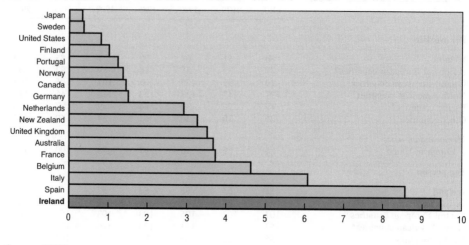

Japan	
Sweden	
United States	
Finland	
Portugal	
Norway	
Canada	
Germany	
Netherlands	
New Zealand	
United Kingdom	
Australia	
France	
Belgium	
Italy	
Spain	
Ireland	

Source: OECD.

interested parties. The government now has to decide on the new structure for the organisation of education and the resources to be allocated to these reforms.[22]

Before investigating the nature and scope of such reforms, the present chapter first looks at the importance of human capital for development in Ireland and its adequacy given the current level of incomes and the level of unemployment. This is followed by a discussion of the strengths and weaknesses of education and training policies in Ireland compared with other Member countries. The chapter concludes by providing some suggestions as to the areas where the reform process should proceed quickly.

Why human capital is essential for Ireland

Human capital – the value of incomes that stem from education, training and other investments in human development – is an important element enabling countries to move from a low to a high level of income. Changes in the global economy currently underline the need for increased accumulation of human capital. Improvements in communications and transport have meant that unskilled workers throughout the world can now be mobilised to compete with the unskilled segment of the domestic labour force. In addition, the demand for labour – be it in the service or manufacturing sector – appears to have been concentrated on those areas that require a well-educated labour force. Such movements have tended to increase the income gap between those with a good education and those with poor qualifications, but even so have resulted in high unemployment amongst the unskilled. Consequently, improvements in the education system are a key element for assuring international competitiveness and long-term growth, as well as for avoiding increased social divisions within the country.

In the case of Ireland, the motivation for reform in education has come from the need to accelerate its transformation from a low-income agricultural country to an industry and service-based economy with incomes similar to the rest of Europe, so minimising currently high levels of emigration. One of the essential components of fast economic growth in Ireland over the past three decades has been a rapid improvement in the average level of education of the workforce. But the rapid growth has not brought about a reduction in unemployment. At least in part, high unemployment has been concentrated amongst those with the lowest level of education, including young people who do not complete the minimum secondary education and older people who did not benefit from free secondary education. By contrast, people with higher levels of human capital have benefited from growth, experiencing unemployment rates at or below those found in the rest of the OECD area. These factors suggest that ensuring an improvement in the quality of education for all will be essential to prevent the unemployment problem from worsening.

Broadening growth

Compared with the rest of Europe, human capital in Ireland is concentrated in certain modern sectors of the economy. High productivity levels are found in the export sector dominated by foreign firms.[23] Although, the usual measures of productivity, such as sales per employee or value added per employee, overstate productivity for a number of reasons (see Box in Part I), modern industries are human-capital intensive, with average earnings 50 per cent higher than in the traditional sector. Moreover, the "modern" sector has few domestic linkages, resulting in a dual economy. This dualism reduces the effective gains from foreign direct investment by slowing down the technological diffusion. The domestic sector consists largely of small, owner-managed firms which offer few internal career development opportunities, thus lowering the incentives of employees to improve their skills. Furthermore, indigenous firms specialise in low-growth sectors, with few learning-by-doing effects. The low productivity performance of the indigenous sector would be improved by increasing the level of human capital of the labour force.

Overall, there appears to be a strong correlation within the OECD area between the growth of human capital and the rate of growth of both labour and total factor productivity. If the growth of human capital is incorporated into a standard production function, this correlation is apparent, and is indeed strengthened, when allowance is made for the process whereby the technology of the leading country is gradually diffused across those that are catching up,[24] so confirming the general importance of education to economic growth. This model of development has been confirmed by several other empirical cross-country studies.[25] On the basis of the overall results of this model, the growth of human capital – as proved by the average ratio of secondary school enrolments to the working population – is estimated to have contributed 0.8 percentage points to the average growth rate of Ireland between 1960 and 1985. The growth of the Irish economy has come without an inordinately rapid growth of conventionally measured factor inputs such as physical capital and labour. Indeed over this period, the growth of total factor productivity (TFP) in Ireland, which includes the impact of human capital formation, proved faster than in any other OECD countries, with the contribution of TFP to the growth performance reaching more than 70 per cent, significantly above the OECD average (Table 20). Moreover, the rapid spread of secondary education over the past two decades may have been one of the reasons which enabled Ireland to avoid the marked slowdown in the growth of productivity seen in most OECD countries after 1974.[26]

Improving income levels

The accumulation of human capital through education, improves a person's "market value" and hence income. While this statistically robust result might reflect employers' use of educational achievement as a screening mechanism, so biasing the apparent returns to education, studies suggest that this is not the

Table 20. **Contributions to output growth**

	1962-1973		1974-1979		1980-1990	
	Ireland	OECD average	**Ireland**	OECD average	**Ireland**	OECD average
Output growth	**4.6**	5.1	**4.1**	2.6	**3.9**	2.6
of which:						
Labour	**-0.1**	0.3	**0.4**	0.2	**-0.2**	0.5
Capital	**1.8**	2.0	**2.0**	1.6	**1.3**	1.1
Total factor productivity	**2.9**	2.7	**1.7**	0.7	**2.8**	1.0

Source: OECD.

case.[27] The income differentials associated with higher education are relatively large in Ireland, suggesting that human capital formation is particularly important. In addition to education, the earnings of individuals are determined by a number of other factors, such as occupational unemployment rates, years of work experience and the number of years that an individual has been out of the labour force.[28] One study shows the gross return to education in Ireland, after allowing for these other factors, to be the second highest in the OECD area, exceeded only by Mexico.[29] In addition, the extent of the increase in the demand for highly qualified labour can be judged from the rise in the earnings differential over different age groups of university graduates. The relative salary of graduates was highest in the youngest age groups, despite the fact that these groups accounted for the largest increase in supply. Overall, the earnings of graduates were 150 per cent higher than those of people with no qualifications beyond the junior secondary level (Table 21).

The relatively high income differentials in favour of those with more education point to a high rate of return on human capital. While there may be reasons why the private and social rates of return could differ, this does suggest that further expansion of the education system would bring a high social yield. The rate of return to education can be calculated in two ways: to private individuals and to society as a whole (the social rate of return). The private rate of return at the university degree level has been estimated at between 14 and 16 per cent,[30] a figure in line with that in other OECD countries (Table 22). The private return for senior secondary education and for sub-degree diplomas was estimated at 10 per

Table 21. **Earnings differentials by education level and age-group**

1987, primary education = 100

	Age group			
	All	15-32	33-49	50-65
Junior secondary cycle	117	115	111	120
Senior secondary cycle	148	142	139	162
Diploma	184	173	160	229
Degree	246	269	218	223

Source: ESRI and DKB (1992).

Table 22. **Rates of return to higher education** [1]

Per cent per annum

	Year of study		Private return		Social return	
	Early study	Later study	Early study	Later study	Early study	Later study
Australia	1969	1976	13.9	21.1	..	16.3
Austria	..	1981	..	4.2	..	..
Belgium	1960	..	8.7	..	6.7	..
Canada	1960	1985	17.4	14.0	14.9	12.1
Denmark	1964	..	10.0	..	7.8	..
France	1962	1976	9.3	20.0	..	..
Germany	1964	1978	4.6	10.5	..	..
Greece	..	1978	14.0	5.5	13.7	4.5
Italy	1969	..	18.3	..	..	..
Japan	1967	1980	10.5	8.8	..	6.9
Korea	1967	1986	..	17.9	5.0	15.5
Mexico	..	1984	21.7	..	..	12.9
New Zealand	1966	1987	14.7	10.6	13.2	7.8
Norway	1966	..	7.7	..	7.5	..
Spain	..	1971	..	15.5	..	12.8
Sweden	1967	..	..	10.3	..	9.2
United Kingdom	..	1978	..	23.0	..	7.0
United States	1970	1987	8.1	9.2	7.4	8.4
Mean	1965	1981	13.2	13.1	9.5	10.3
Memorandum item:						
Ireland	..	**1987**	..	**16.0**	..	**12.0** [2]

1. The estimates of rates of return in this table have been drawn from a large number of independent studies which may have used somewhat different methodologies.
2. OECD estimate.
Source: Psacharopoulos (1993), "Returns to investment in education, a global update", *World Bank Working Papers*, No. 1067 and DKB consultants (1993) for Ireland.

cent. Part of the higher private return to degree-level education may reflect the payment of maintenance grants. As a result, the social return to different levels of education may be lower than the private return. It is more difficult, though, to calculate the social rate of return in Ireland as a large portion of the labour force emigrates each year, resulting in lost income to Ireland.[31] Nevertheless, if there is an overall cash constraint on the education budget, the social rate of return on secondary education and sub-degree courses should be evaluated. Funds could then be allocated in a way which maximise returns, given the budget constraint. An alternative to calculating the social rate of return would be to consider the rate of return to the government.[32] On the basis of the current system of financing higher education and current income and indirect tax rates, this measure would appear to be around 12 per cent,[33] which is higher than the rate of return on government bonds and the long-run private rate of return on equities.

In contrast to the high earnings of the well-educated, those people leaving school with poor qualifications receive relatively low levels of earnings. Indeed, after only one year in the labour market,[34] there is a wide gap between those with a good education (as measured by the grade obtained in the school-leaving certificates) and those who have either not taken the examination at the end of the junior secondary cycle or who have only obtained poor results (Diagram 13). In 1990, the market value of school-leavers who had not completed the lower secondary cycle was about Ir£ 1.60 per hour.

Absorbing the labour surplus

The unemployment rate has increased faster in Ireland than in other countries since the early 1970s (Diagram 14). Moreover, as noted, unemployment has tended to be more long-term in nature than in other countries, and is associated with low levels of human capital, with more than two-thirds of the jobless in 1992 having had only a primary or junior secondary school education (Table 23). In contrast, the unemployment rate for those who finished secondary school or had a third-level qualification was, at that time, relatively low. The correlation, though, between the level of education and the unemployment rate is seen primarily amongst the long-term unemployed; the rate for those with only a primary education is more than five times higher than those with a diploma (Table 24). The human capital of the poorly educated is further eroded by their long periods of inactivity. On the other hand, the rate of short-term unemploy-

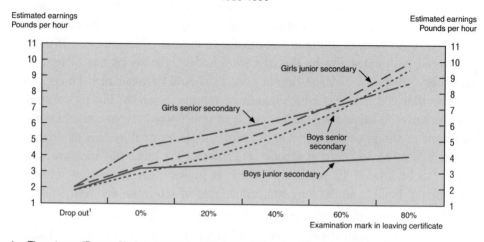

Diagram 13. **QUALITY OF EDUCATION AND EARNINGS**

Estimated earnings of pupils one year after leaving school
1988-1990

Estimated earnings
Pounds per hour

Estimated earnings
Pounds per hour

Girls junior secondary

Girls senior secondary

Boys senior
secondary

Boys junior secondary

Drop out¹   0%   20%   40%   60%   80%

Examination mark in leaving certificate

1. The category "Drop out" includes all those who failed to sit the relevant leaving certiticate.
Source: Breen and Hannan (1993).

Diagram 14. **THE RISE IN UNEMPLOYMENT**

Rise compared with the average unemployment rate of the 1960s

Percentage points

Percentage points

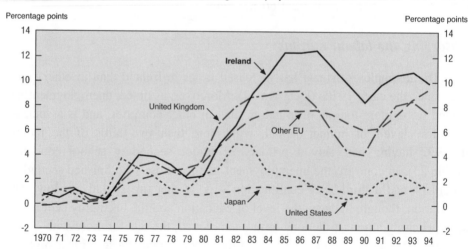

Ireland

United Kingdom

Other EU

Japan

United States

1970 71 72 73 74 75 76 77 78 79 80 81 82 83 84 85 86 87 88 89 90 91 92 93 94

Source: OECD.

Table 23. **Unemployment by educational level and age**

	15-24	25-29	30-34	35-44	45-54	55-64	Total
Unemployment rate							
(per cent)							
Primary	45.1	39.5	38.0	27.2	18.6	10.4	24.1
Junior secondary	28.7	21.6	19.9	16.6	11.4	9.1	19.9
Senior secondary	12.0	10.4	8.8	9.6	8.3	4.5	10.9
Diploma	15.2	6.6	5.3	5.7	4.0	3.7	7.5
Degree	12.5	4.8	3.3	2.4	2.8	1.9	4.1
Total	21.8	14.9	14.4	14.4	11.8	8.0	15.1
Numbers unemployed							
Primary	10 700	6 800	7 900	20 400	15 200	6 300	67 300
Junior secondary	26 500	12 300	11 300	15 000	5 600	1 800	72 500
Senior secondary	19 000	7 900	5 700	8 000	3 600	800	45 000
Diploma	4 600	1 800	1 200	200	800	300	10 700
Degree	1 700	1 100	700	900	700	200	5 300
Total	62 500	29 900	26 800	46 300	25 900	9 400	200 800

Source: Labour Force Survey (1992), unpublished CSO, Dublin.

ment is similar for all levels of educational attainment. Overall, however, the gap between the total unemployment rate of those with low educational qualifications and those with a university degree in Ireland is high relative to other countries

Table 24. **Unemployment by educational level and duration**

Education level	Short Duration Less than one year		Long Duration More than one year		Total	
	Numbers	Rate[1] (per cent)	Numbers	Rate (per cent)	Numbers	Rate (per cent)
Primary	17 200	6.2	50 100	17.9	67 300	24.1
Junior secondary	28 300	7.8	44 200	12.1	72 500	19.9
Senior secondary	22 600	5.5	22 400	5.4	45 000	10.9
Diploma	6 000	4.2	4 700	3.3	10 700	7.5
Degree	3 300	2.5	2 000	1.5	5 300	4.1
Total	77 400	5.8	123 400	9.3	200 800	15.1

1. The denominator of this rate is the *total* labour force with a given educational qualification.
Source: Labour Force Survey 1992 (unpublished) CSO, Dublin.

Diagram 15. **UNEMPLOYMENT DIFFERENTIALS BY EDUCATION LEVEL**[1]

1991

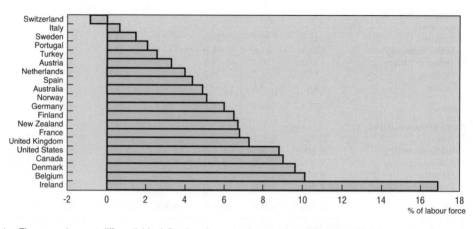

1. The unemployment differential is defined as the unemployment rate of persons with a lower secondary and primary school level education less that of university graduates.
Source: OECD.

(Diagram 15), suggesting that the Irish labour market for unskilled workers does not function well. One reason may be the availability of long-term unemployment benefits:[35] in countries where there is no correlation between education and unemployment rates, such as Portugal, Sweden, Spain and Italy, unemployment benefits are limited to a maximum of three years.

Failure or low achievement at school also worsens the transition from school to work. Although the number with low qualifications is falling, almost one-fifth of all pupils left school in 1992 with only a Junior Certificate while another 6 per cent left without qualifications (Table 25).[36] The initial labour market experience of the latter group is especially poor (Table 26). One year after leaving school, this group has an unemployment rate of almost 50 per cent and accounts for over 10 per cent of unemployment amongst a given school-leaving cohort.[37] The close correlation between unemployment and education extends not only to the level of qualification but also to the quality of the results, as measured by the average grade obtained[38] (Diagram 16). High unemployment amongst poorly-educated

Table 25. **Qualifications of school leavers**

	1979/80	1983/84	1987/88	1989/90	1991/92
	Percentage distribution				
No qualifications	9.1	8.1	6.8	6.1	6.6
Junior secondary	26.7	25.0	22.9	18.1	17.3
Senior secondary	64.2	66.9	70.3	75.8	76.1
	Numbers				
No qualifications	5 800	5 000	4 500	4 000	4 400
Junior secondary	17 100	15 400	15 400	12 100	11 600
Senior secondary	41 300	41 300	47 300	50 900	51 000

Source: Annual School leavers Survey. Department of Enterprise and Employment and ESRI, Dublin.

Table 26. **Unemployment rate of pupils one year after leaving school**
Per cent of cohort

Educational qualification	1979/80	1983/84	1987/88	1989/90	1991/92[1]
No qualifications	26.8	57.0	59.9	52.4	49.0
Junior secondary	12.6	27.2	34.1	31.8	39.2
Senior secondary	10.4	34.3	20.9	23.7	25.8
Total	13.5	37.8	29.5	29.0	35.1

1. The figures exclude those on government schemes. In 1991/92 the total number on schemes was 6.7 percent of the labour force.
Source: Annual School Leavers Survey.

people imposes considerable social costs and also adds considerably to government expenditure.

The opportunities for education are very unevenly distributed across Irish society, suggesting that there may be substantial possibilities to raise the average level of human capital by redirecting educational resources towards lower socioeconomic groups. Participation in higher education varies by income level.[39] Between 1991 and 1993, children from higher socio-economic backgrounds[40] had an average participation rate of 57 per cent – more than double that of children from other backgrounds (Diagram 17). The disparity, which was even greater amongst students enrolled in universities, results from three factors. *First,* nearly 90 per cent of the children of higher-status families stay at school for the senior

Diagram 16. **QUALITY OF EDUCATION AND UNEMPLOYMENT**

Estimated unemployment rate of pupils one year after leaving school

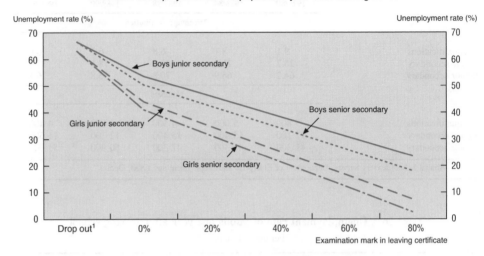

1. The category "Drop out" includes all those who failed to sit the relevant leaving certificate.
Source: Breen and Hannan (1993).

Diagram 17. **EDUCATIONAL PARTICIPATION ACCORDING TO FATHER'S JOB**

% of a cohort enrolled in higher education

1991-1993

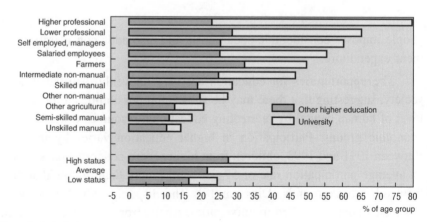

Source: Clancy (forthcoming).

secondary cycle as opposed to only 68 per cent for the rest of the population. *Second,* in secondary schools, the academic results of children from lower-status families are poorer. *Third,* the proportion of pupils from lower-status groups who access higher education is lower than is the case for children with equivalent academic results from higher-status backgrounds (except those very able children who go on to higher education regardless of background).

Meeting skill needs

Because of the high returns to human capital, there do not appear to be specific skill shortages. The job vacancy ratio does not point to any specific skills mismatch, which would simultaneously generate persistent unemployment in some areas and unfilled vacancies in others. In addition, surveys of Irish employers do not point to a shortage of skilled labour. The fact that a significant proportion of new graduates emigrate, even in high-tech industrial sectors such as electronics, also suggests that there is not a skill shortage.[41] Indeed, the integration of the Irish labour market with that of the United Kingdom is another factor that has enabled Ireland to avoid skill shortages. When the domestic labour market is confronted with a lack of particular skills, employers always have the option of "hiring them home from Britain".[42]

Nevertheless, international comparisons show a much lower level of skills in Irish firms compared with those abroad.[43] Employment in Irish manufacturing is characterised by a larger proportion of unskilled or semi-skilled personnel than in other European countries, with twice as many "unqualified" staff as in Germany (Table 27). However, as noted above, the shortfall is at the level of intermediate qualifications rather than in highly-qualified staff. Irish companies suffer from a shortage of basic production skills at the operating level which is partly a consequence of a lack of technical knowledge at the supervisory and managerial level.[44] Consequently, "one of the basic requirements in the effort to upgrade production skills is a better appreciation, among Irish industrial managers, of the importance of higher skill standards and a better understanding of what such standards consist of".[45] The problem may, thus, not be so much a shortage of supply but a lack of demand for human capital in some businesses. Matched comparisons of Irish plants with foreign counterparts suggest that productivity may also be affected by a lack of diversity of skills.[46]

67

Table 27. **Comparative skill levels in Irish industry**[1]

	Germany	Ireland	United Kingdom	N. Ireland
Graduates	100	**88**	110	45
Technician	100	**100**	53	49
Craftsmen	100	**51**	47	60
Unqualified	100	**196**	212	180

1. Technicians: Irish figures unlikely to match other in depth of study. Craftsmen: Irish figure inflated by inclusion of non-vocational qualifications. The figures show the proportion of the manufacturing labour force with each qualification as its highest qualification compared to the proportion in German manufacturing industry.
Source: NESC, Dublin.

In sum, the Irish education system could further aid economic development in a number of areas. An increase in the average level of human capital of the working population would speed-up the convergence of Irish incomes towards those of the more prosperous countries in Europe. This requires improving the access to education for the disadvantaged groups of society. In order to address the problems of high unemployment and a low earning potential, an improvement in the average level of education will need to be accompanied by a rapid reduction in the numbers of those who currently leave school with low qualifications. Improving the education of this group of students, though, will not significantly reduce unemployment unless it is accompanied by significant labour market reforms (See Part III). The next section looks more closely at areas of the education system where quantitative and qualitative reforms could improve the Irish performance relative to its international competitors.

The role of the education system

Main features of the system

Education in Ireland is a co-operative effort between central and local governments and a number of private organisations, primarily of a religious nature.[47] *Primary education* is provided almost exclusively by schools which are owned by a religious patron and are denominational in character. Nevertheless, the government controls curricula and student assessment and establishes regulations for management, staffing, organisation and physical facilities.[48] Although the mandatory age for starting this cycle is six, nearly all children have begun school by five. Children usually transfer to the secondary cycle following their twelfth birthday, with parents having the right to select the school of their choice. *Secondary education,* which has consisted of a three-year lower cycle followed by a two-year upper cycle, is provided in four types of schools. About 60 per cent of students are enrolled in *secondary schools,* which are privately-owned and managed institutions, nearly all by religious authorities. A quarter of secondary pupils attend *vocational schools,* controlled by a local government organisation. The remainder of secondary pupils are in *comprehensive* and *community schools,* which combine academic and vocational subjects under the direct control of the Department of Education. All pupils take a national examination (the Junior Certificate) at the end of the first three-year cycle and those who remain until the end of the second cycle take a second examination (the Leaving Certificate). In addition to a general academic curriculum, vocational schools offer more practical courses to those who have finished the normal secondary cycles. *Tertiary education* includes both university and non-university programmes. There are four universities and five teacher training colleges. Sub-degree higher education is provided in eleven regional technical colleges and the Dublin Institute of Technology.

Although most primary and secondary schools are privately owned, they are financed almost entirely by the government. The owner of a school is only responsible for raising about 5 per cent of total running costs, but when a new school is constructed, the owner has to supply the land and pay 15 per cent of building costs.[49] There is central control over teachers' salaries, recruitment and determination of the size of the staff as well as assessment of teaching. Higher education is controlled by a special government authority which provides financing. Tuition fees have been set at a level which covers about one-third of the universities' costs and an even lower proportion of the costs of technical colleges. However, about half of all students have received grants covering these fees in addition to maintenance grants.[50] Beginning in the autumn of 1995, 50 per cent of fees will be paid by the central government and from the autumn of 1996, fees will no longer be charged. For technical colleges, a significant portion of these funds are provided by the European Commission through European Social Fund Training Grants which cover one-third of the costs of higher education grants.

The expansion of the system

Education has been a major priority of the Irish government. Its share of total government expenditure has risen from 16 per cent in 1965 to 20 per cent in 1993, while the number of students rose by almost 50 per cent. The effort to expand and improve the school system during the past three decades has led to a sharp increase in the level of education of school leavers and a more gradual rise in that of the population as a whole. The growing number of students in post-primary education accounted for most of the increase in the student population. Between 1965 and 1992, the number of secondary-level students rose by a factor of 2.5 while that of tertiary students quadrupled, reflecting both increased enrolment rates and demographic trends (Diagram 18). During the same period, the proportion participating in full-time education rose from 50 to 100 per cent for 15 year-olds, and from 25 to 66 per cent for 17 year-olds. Primary enrolment was already complete in the early 1960s, so that movements in the number of pupils since then have been determined by demographic factors. An abrupt decline in the birth rate in the early 1980s led to a fall in primary school numbers beginning in 1985. By 1991, enrolment had fallen back to the level of the early 1960s.

Diagram 18. **NUMBER OF STUDENTS**

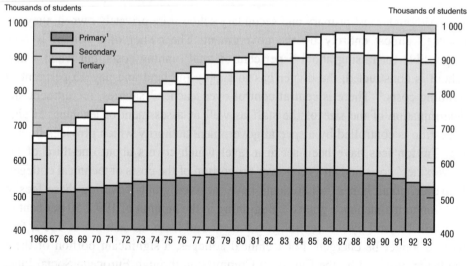

1. Includes pre-primary students.
Source: Department of Education.

70

During the first stages of the quantitative expansion of the education system, expenditure on education rose rapidly, from 3.2 per cent of GNP in 1965 to over 6 per cent by 1983. Following expenditure cuts in the mid-1980s, the share dropped to around 5 per cent before returning to 6.5 per cent of GNP by 1993 (Diagram 19). This stability of expenditure relative to GNP is the result of offsetting productivity trends that occurred at different levels of education. Productivity has risen in higher education in the past decade as the number of students per lecturer increased by 37 per cent in the universities and 55 per cent in the RTC/DIT sector. In primary and secondary schools, costs have risen markedly as the number of pupils per teacher fell to 27 in 1991 and to about 21 in 1994 (Diagram 20). Despite the sharp decline, the ratio in Ireland remained higher than the OECD average of 18.

In 1991, the share of GNP devoted to education in Ireland was the same as for the average of OECD countries. Ireland, though, has almost twice as many pupils relative to the number of people employed as in rest of the OECD area. As a result, Irish expenditure per pupil is much lower than the OECD average, even when compared to GNP per person employed in order to take into account lower

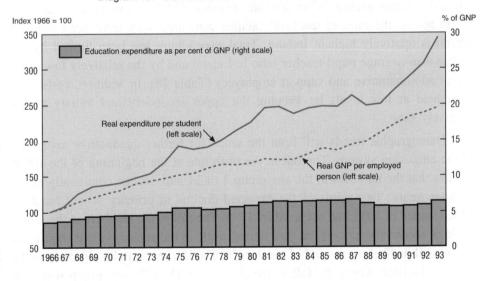

Diagram 19. **GOVERNMENT EXPENDITURE IN EDUCATION**

Index 1966 = 100

% of GNP

Education expenditure as per cent of GNP (right scale)

Real expenditure per student (left scale)

Real GNP per employed person (left scale)

1966 67 68 69 70 71 72 73 74 75 76 77 78 79 80 81 82 83 84 85 86 87 88 89 90 91 92 93

Source: Ministry of Finance.

Diagram 20. **NUMBER OF PUPILS AND PUPIL TEACHER RATIO**
PRIMARY SCHOOLS
1985 = 100

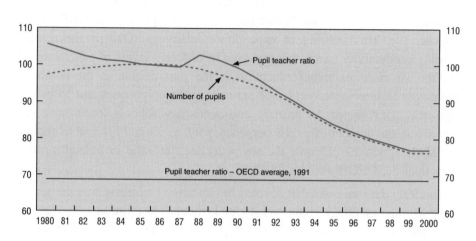

Source: Department of Education and OECD.

incomes in Ireland. Indeed, Irish educational expenditure per pupil is about two-thirds the simple average of such a ratio in other OECD countries (Diagram 21). Nevertheless, the ratio of teachers' salaries compared with GNP per employed person is relatively high in Ireland. Total expenditure has been limited by the higher-than-average pupil-teacher ratio in Ireland and by the relatively low number of administrative and support employees (Table 28). In addition, costs have been held at low levels by keeping the upper secondary and tertiary cycles relatively short.

Demographic trends will limit the scope for further quantitative expansion of the education system. The fall in the birth rate at the beginning of the 1980s implies that the numbers in the age group 4 to 24 will decline continually in the next ten years. Two-thirds of the expected decline in primary school numbers which started in 1987 had occurred by 1995. The fall in the numbers in the junior cycle of secondary schools has just started while in the senior cycle it should not begin until just before the end of the decade. The last sector to be affected will be higher education where the fall in the size of the 18 to 21 age group will only start after the year 2000. Given these trends, maintaining educational enrolments

Diagram 21. **EDUCATIONAL COSTS**

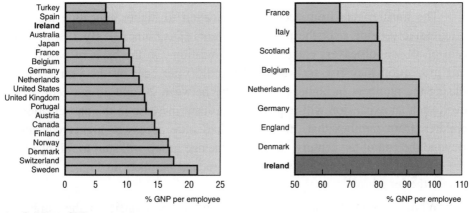

A. Expenditure per pupil, 1991[1]

Turkey
Spain
Ireland
Australia
Japan
France
Belgium
Germany
Netherlands
United States
United Kingdom
Portugal
Austria
Canada
Finland
Norway
Denmark
Switzerland
Sweden

0   5   10   15   20   25

% GNP per employee

B. Teachers salaries 1988[1]

France
Italy
Scotland
Belgium
Netherlands
Germany
England
Denmark
Ireland

50   60   70   80   90   100   110

% GNP per employee

1.   Relative to GNP per employee.
Source: Department of Education and OECD.

Table 28.   **Distribution of educational costs**

1991
Per cent of total costs

	Teachers salaries	Other salaries	Total	Other costs
Ireland	**75.7**	**8.2**	**83.9**	**16.1**
Australia	55.1	14.9	70.0	30.0
Austria	51.7	15.1	66.8	33.2
Canada	46.4	17.0	63.4	36.6
Denmark	53.2	14.5	67.7	32.3
Finland	50.7	15.6	66.3	33.7
Japan	46.9	14.3	61.2	38.9
Norway	58.9	14.6	73.5	26.5
Portugal	85.4	3.0	88.4	11.7
Switzerland	61.2	13.8	75.0	25.0
Turkey	86.5	6.5	93.0	7.0
United Kingdom	51.3	16.6	67.9	32.1
Mean	60.3	12.8	73.1	26.9
France	..	..	72.1	27.9
Germany	..	..	74.3	25.7
Netherlands	..	..	69.0	31.0

Source: OECD.

will require higher participation rates. In the senior secondary sector, the rise in participation rates to 78 per cent in 1994 suggests that the scope for further increase is limited. The government intends that 90 per cent of children should complete the senior secondary cycle by the end of the century.

The transfer rate from secondary education to higher education has been progressively rising over the past fifteen years (Diagram 22). By 1994, 38 per cent of all school-leavers entered higher education. On the basis of past trends, this proportion may rise to between 45 and 50 per cent by the year 2000, so raising the numbers in higher education by between 20 and 30 per cent. However, such an expansion will require a significant increase in the participation of children from families that, in the past, had little access to higher education. Beyond the end of the century, the size of the age group will start to fall by about 3¹/₂ per cent per year which will tend to reduce numbers in higher education unless the length of courses rises.

While demographic factors are going to limit the expansion in the number of new secondary and university graduates in the next decade, there will still be a

Diagram 22. **PARTICIPATION IN HIGHER EDUCATION**

Percentage of age group entering higher education

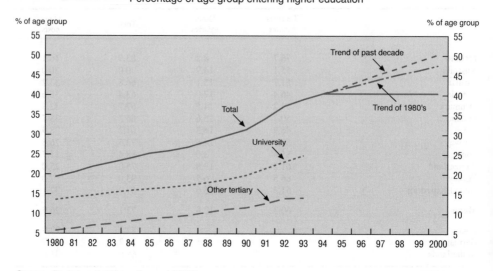

Source: Department of Education and OECD.

74

considerable improvement in the average human capital of the labour force over the next two generations. This will occur because of the large difference between the qualifications of the new entrants to the labour market and the qualifications of those retiring. Indeed, it has been estimated by the Secretariat that Ireland will experience the third most rapid increase in human capital in the OECD area over the next thirty years[51] (Table 29). In addition, the improvement in educational standards will probably be associated with an increase in the labour force participation rate of women, as experience in the rest of the OECD area suggests that female participation rates rise with the level of education. Such a trend would further reduce the gap between per capita incomes in Ireland and the rest of Europe.

Table 29. **Estimated increase in human capital**

1991 to 2020

	Graduation rate			Qualified stock			Estimated increase in human capital Per cent
	Secondary	Diploma	University	Secondary	Diploma	University	
	Per cent of cohort			Per cent of population			
Ireland	**47**	**15**	**16**	**24**	**8**	**8**	**18**
Spain	45	0	20	12	0	10	25
Australia	46	11	24	25	21	6	19
Turkey	20	1	7	11	0	6	15
Italy	42	0	9	22	0	6	13
France	51	9	16	35	5	10	12
Finland	68	15	17	42	8	10	10
Netherlands	59	15	8	37	13	6	7
Norway	53	18	19	54	12	12	7
Denmark	74	9	17	43	6	13	7
Belgium	55	12	13	24	10	10	6
United Kingdom	49	7	18	49	7	10	6
Sweden	38	30	12	44	11	12	5
Austria	77	2	8	61	0	7	4
United States	24	20	30	47	13	24	4
Germany	83	4	13	60	11	11	2
Switzerland	73	7	8	60	13	7	0
Canada	39	n.a.	33	36	23	17	n.a.
Japan	39	28	24	0	0	0	n.a.
New Zealand	19	n.a.	16	33	13	10	n.a.
Portugal	51	n.a.	n.a.	3	1	3	n.a.

Source: OECD.

The performance of the system

The expansion of secondary and tertiary education has meant that the level of human capital of the working population has improved considerably. Despite this improvement, the level of educational attainment among the adult population in 1991 was still low in Ireland compared with other OECD countries, reflecting the relatively late development of post-primary education (Table 30). Indeed, only four OECD countries – Turkey, Spain, Portugal and Italy – had a higher proportion of the adult population having stopped at the first cycle of secondary education. Only 40 per cent of adults in Ireland had completed upper secondary

Table 30. **Level of educational attainment**

Percentage of population in 1991 by age group that had received at least the given level of education

Population aged	Lower secondary education		Upper secondary education		Non-university tertiary education		University education	
	25-34	25-64	25-34	25-64	25-34	25-64	25-34	25-64
European Community								
Belgium	87	73	58	44	27	20	13	10
Denmark	100	100	74	61	19	18	13	12
France	100	100	66	51	20	15	12	10
Germany	100	100	90	82	22	22	12	12
Ireland	**87**	**67**	**55**	**40**	**20**	**16**	**9**	**8**
Italy	90	61	43	28	6	6	6	6
Netherlands	90	81	67	55	22	19	6	6
Portugal	20	13	12	7	6	4	4	3
Spain	69	37	40	22	16	10	16	10
United Kingdom	100	100	79	65	19	16	12	9
Other Europe-OECD								
Austria	100	100	80	68	8	7	8	7
Finland	100	100	82	60	21	18	11	10
Norway	100	100	88	79	27	25	12	12
Sweden	100	100	92	67	25	23	10	11
Switzerland	100	100	87	80	21	20	9	7
Turkey	32	25	22	17	6	6	6	6
North America								
Canada	96	89	86	76	44	40	17	17
United States	96	93	87	83	38	36	24	23
Pacific area								
Australia	97	86	65	56	36	31	13	10
New Zealand	13	67	59	56	23	23	12	10
Country mean	87	79	66	55	21	19	11	10

Source: OECD, *Education at a Glance* (1993).

school, a figure substantially below the mean of 55 per cent in the OECD area. Moreover, by 1991, even with the expansion of education in recent years, the level of educational attainment by young adults (25 to 34 years of age) was significantly less than the average of the OECD area. In 1991, only 55 per cent of this group had completed the upper cycle of secondary school compared with a 66 per cent average in the OECD countries. The difference was most pronounced for young men, where the proportion completing the upper cycle of secondary education was only 50 per cent, compared to 60 per cent for women. However, since this cohort of adults had, on average, completed the upper secondary cycle in 1979 these figures do not reflect the improvements in educational attainments that have taken place recently. By 1991, for example, the proportion of the relevant age group graduating from the upper cycle of secondary education had risen to 78 per cent, and to 85 per cent for women, somewhat above the OECD average.

The expansion in higher education still leaves Ireland with a lower proportion of its population with a degree or diploma than the average of OECD countries. The share has risen from 5 per cent in 1971 to 16 per cent in 1991 but this is still lower than the OECD average of about 20 per cent. By 1991, as with secondary education, the proportion of a given age cohort completing studies in the university and other tertiary sectors was similar to the OECD average of about 31 per cent. However, although a considerably lower proportion of the age group enters higher education, this is compensated by a low failure rate in Ireland.

While the proportion of youths completing the upper cycle of secondary education is now comparable to those in other OECD countries, the shortness of both the senior secondary cycle and the university cycle means that a relatively low proportion of the over 17 age group is in full-time education (Diagram 23). Prior to the 1994 academic year when the cycle was lengthened, most students finished the secondary programme in Ireland at age 17, compared with a range of 18 to 20 in other countries. Consequently, most students finished the three-year degree courses at age 20, five years after the end of the junior secondary cycle, as opposed to seven years in most European countries. As a result, the educational participation rates fell more rapidly after age 17 in Ireland than in other countries. The participation rate at age 18 was similar to that elsewhere at 20, while the participation rate at 20 was equivalent to that at 22 elsewhere. Indeed, the shorter

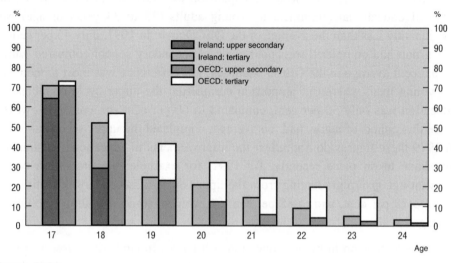

Diagram 23. **ENROLMENT IN SECONDARY AND HIGHER EDUCATION**
Percentage of age group, 1991

Source: OECD.

upper secondary and tertiary cycle has been an important method by which total costs have been controlled.

International comparisons, dating from 1991, also show that Irish pupils tend to rank below average in standardised tests, although the extent of the shortfall is small in mathematics and reading. In mathematics, the average score of Irish 13 year-olds was 3 per cent below the mean of the thirteen countries shown in Diagram 24.[52] Large margins of error, though, are associated with these test results. Consequently, the scores of only four countries – Hungary, Switzerland, Taiwan and Korea – were significantly superior to Ireland. In reading, Irish 14 year-olds scored 3 per cent below the average of 22 countries, with eleven countries significantly superior to Ireland. Science was the weakest area for Irish students, reflecting the lack of emphasis given to this subject in primary schools. Ireland's score was 9 per cent below the average, and significantly worse than every other country shown in Diagram 24 with the exception of Portugal. If these results are aggregated for the ten countries for which mathematics, reading and science scores are available, Ireland ranks eighth,

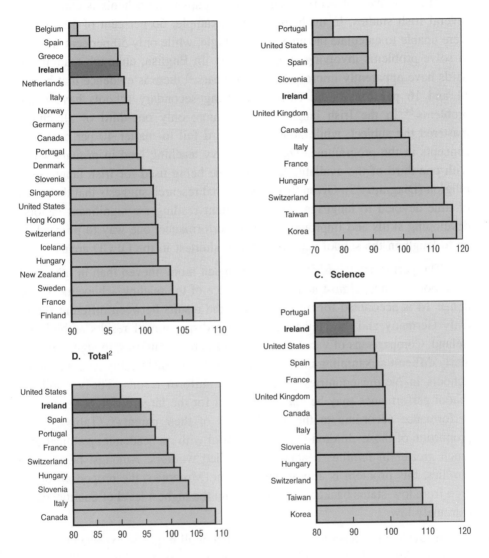

Diagram 24. **COMPARISON OF EDUCATIONAL ABILITY**
Age 13, international average = 100

A. Reading[1]

Belgium
Spain
Greece
Ireland
Netherlands
Italy
Norway
Germany
Canada
Portugal
Denmark
Slovenia
Singapore
United States
Hong Kong
Switzerland
Iceland
Hungary
New Zealand
Sweden
France
Finland

90   95   100   105   110

B. Mathematics

Portugal
United States
Spain
Slovenia
Ireland
United Kingdom
Canada
Italy
France
Hungary
Switzerland
Taiwan
Korea

70   80   90   100   110   120

C. Science

Portugal
Ireland
United States
Spain
France
United Kingdom
Canada
Italy
Slovenia
Hungary
Switzerland
Taiwan
Korea

80   90   100   110   120

D. Total[2]

United States
Ireland
Spain
Portugal
France
Switzerland
Hungary
Slovenia
Italy
Canada

80   85   90   95   100   105   110

1. Age 14.
2. Simple average of test results for those countries in which all three subject results are available.
Source: IAEAA and IAEP.

79

about $3\frac{1}{2}$ per cent below the average. Moreover, the results of the lowest decile of pupils is even worse, falling to almost 10 per cent below the international average.

The low level of achievement of some pupils and schools is confirmed by several Irish studies. In mathematics, for example, 60 per cent of 12 year-olds were unable to calculate the area of a rectangle, while only 50 per cent were able to solve problems involving simple interest. In English, although reading standards have apparently improved over the years,[53] there is evidence that between 11 and 16 per cent of all children entering secondary schools have reading problems.[54] In the Irish language programme, only one-third of all children mastered the subject, while another one-third fail to master 40 per cent of the concepts in the programme. There is a heavy teaching load in primary schools with one-third of the available teaching time being used for Irish language and religion (Diagram 25). Given that international research suggests that the amount of time devoted to language study and silent reading are significant factors in developing skills and improving reading performance, one way to proceed may be to lengthen the school year, the second shortest in the OECD area.

The performance of Irish schools is much more uneven than in other countries. For instance, almost half of the variance of the reading achievement scores at age 14 is accounted for by variation in the results between different schools. Only Germany and the Netherlands have a dispersion of results as high as in Ireland. Comparisons of variability of results across countries, though, are particularly difficult as sampling methods and sizes vary considerably across countries. Schools in Nordic countries produce very uniform results. The variability of school performance may be one explanation for the large differences in student performance according to the social status of their parents[55] (Table 31). The proportion of those children who leave school with no academic qualifications is much greater in families headed by unskilled workers. Amongst higher status families, this problem is almost non-existent. Moreover, the proportion of children from low-status backgrounds that obtain the highest level of qualifications is extremely low.

A low level of resources devoted to each pupil might be expected to result in a low quality level, if education were similar to any other production process. Whether this relationship holds in education has been a matter of some controversy. One study found a positive relationship between school quality (as proxied

Diagram 25. **USE OF PRIMARY SCHOOL TEACHING TIME**

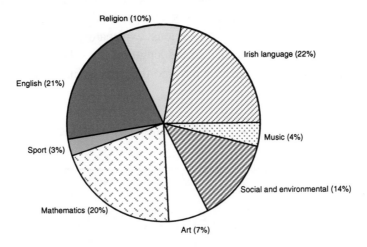

- Religion (10%)
- Irish language (22%)
- English (21%)
- Music (4%)
- Sport (3%)
- Social and environmental (14%)
- Mathematics (20%)
- Art (7%)

Source: Department of Education.

Table 31. **Educational performance and family background** [1]

	No qualification	Junior cycle	Senior cycle		
			Level 1	Level 2	Level 3
Unskilled manual	16.2	31.2	29.4	19.0	4.1
Other agricultural	12.3	24.7	27.9	22.2	10.7
Semi-skilled manual	9.9	28.4	33.9	22.4	6.1
Other non-manual	7.7	21.7	29.4	32.4	8.7
Skilled manual	5.9	18.1	30.6	35.9	9.4
Intermediate non-manual	3.5	11.9	20.2	46.2	17.9
Farmers	2.7	13.9	20.2	46.5	16.7
Self employed, managers	1.8	7.8	17.0	46.7	27.2
salaried employees	1.6	4.7	21.8	44.7	26.7
Lower professional	0.4	3.4	10.2	45.4	40.1
Higher professional	0.0	2.9	6.8	37.0	52.9
Low status	9.0	22.6	30.1	30.3	8.0
Average	5.7	16.3	24.0	37.4	16.7
High status	2.0	9.3	17.1	45.2	26.3

1. No qualification indicates failure to complete the junior cycle;
   Junior certificate is the junior secondary cycle leaving examination;
   Level 1 corresponds to ordinary passes at the senior cycle leaving examination;
   Level 2 corresponds to up to 4 higher level passes;
   Level 3 corresponds to 5 or more higher passes.
Source: Clancey (forthcoming).

81

by the pupil-teacher ratio, relative pay of teachers and the length of the school year) and the returns to education.[56] The results of cross-country performance tests in mathematics and science can be compared with the variation in inputs. A regression of the test results on various explanatory variables confirms that performance is positively related to the length of the school year but negatively related to the length of the school day and the average class size[57] (Diagram 26).

Diagram 26. **QUALITY OF EDUCATION AND RESOURCE INPUTS**[1]

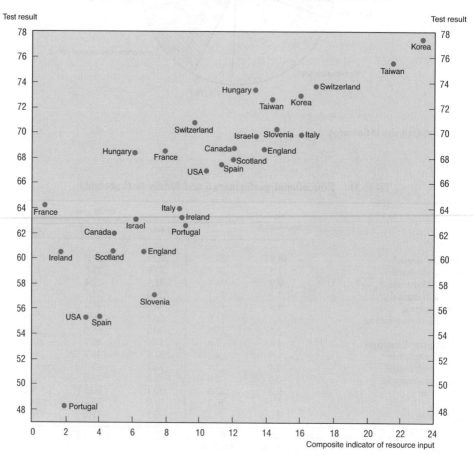

1. The scatter diagram shows the relationship between scores in mathematics and science in internationaly comparable tests and a weighted average of educational inputs (class size, length of school year, length of school day).
Source: OECD.

Table 32. **Irish educational inputs**

		Fifteen country average[1]	Ireland	Percentage difference
Class size	Pupils	24.8	**27.0**	8.9
Length of school year	Days	192.9	**173.0**	−10.3
Length of school day	Minutes	300.2	**323.0**	7.6

1. Sample of fifteen countries covered by the IAEA standardized educational tests.
Source: International Association for Education Avancement (IAEA).

Such results are only indicative as there are many other variables that enter into the determination of educational performance. The poor performance of Irish pupils on standardised educational tests might then be explained by the low level of inputs into education in Ireland resulting from the short school year and the large class size (Table 32). The low inputs appear to be offset to some extent by factors such as the high quality of teachers[58] as the actual performance of Irish students is somewhat above that predicted by the model.

The contribution of vocational education

The relatively low emphasis on vocational education and training in Ireland reflects the priority given to general education up to the age of 18. This appears to be supported by research which emphasises the acquisition of transferable skills at school, leaving the acquisition of employment-related qualifications for later. A range of studies suggests that in many countries the social rate of return seems to be higher on general education than on vocational education at the secondary level, with little difference being found in the private rate of return[59] (Table 33). In 1991, only 22 per cent of Irish upper secondary school students

Table 33. **Average returns to different types of secondary education across countries**[1]

Curriculum type	Rate of return	
	Social	Private
Academic/general	15.5	11.7
Technical/vocational	10.6	10.5

1. The returns have been estimated from a sample of mainly developing countries.
Source: Psacharopoulos (1993).

83

were involved in vocational education and apprenticeship programmes, compared with a mean of almost 50 per cent in OECD countries generally. Although the proportion in Ireland is similar to other English-speaking countries and Japan, it is substantially below some European countries where 75 per cent of upper secondary students are in such programmes. However, such measures tend to understate the extent of vocationally-related education in Ireland. The proportion of children following scientific, technical or applied linguistic subjects within the so-called general stream of education has been rising steadily. This is reflected in a higher proportion of mathematics, science and engineering graduates than in nearly all other OECD countries. Moreover, the proportion of scientific graduates in the 25 to 34 age group is second only to Japan and is nearly 40 per cent above the mean in the OECD area despite a very high rate of emigration. In addition, the expansion of sub-degree higher education has been concentrated in the area of technical studies.

The importance of training

Private sector initiatives

The evidence on the extent of private sector training is limited. Estimates dating from 1989 suggest that about 8 per cent of the labour force received four days a year of off-the-job training, rising to 15 per cent for professional staff (Table 34). Overall, Irish companies devoted the equivalent of 0.9 per cent of payroll costs to training compared with 1.4 per cent in the United States, 2.1 per cent in France and 2.9 per cent in Germany.[60] However, more recent information, from the 1992 EU Labour Force survey suggests that the Irish training effort is not as low as suggested by estimates based on training costs. According to the survey, the training rate in Ireland (as measured by the proportion of respondents who replied that they had been trained in the previous four weeks) was only slightly below the EU average (Table 35). The extent of training conducted exclusively within the firm was considerably higher than in the EU. If the comparison is extended to training that is undertaken jointly by the employer and the education system, then the Irish training rate is still above the EU average. The only area where the survey showed Ireland to be markedly below the EU average was in training undertaken as part of general education or in institutes of

Table 34. **The extent of training**

1989

Per cent of workers trained in last year

Occupation	Type of training				
	On job	Off job			Total
		Total	Up to 3 days	4 days or more	
Management	7.6	30.9	20.8	10.1	38.5
Supervisor	17.6	26.0	13.1	12.9	43.7
Professional	6.1	44.4	29.2	15.2	50.5
Technician	16.3	30.3	21.2	9.1	46.6
Craftsman	20.4	13.1	6.6	6.5	33.5
Apprentice	27.0	65.7	0.7	65.0	92.7
Operatives	37.8	9.4	6.3	3.1	47.2
Clerical	16.8	26.4	18.2	8.2	43.2
Sales	18.6	12.8	9.3	3.4	31.3
Public employees	11.5	21.7	18.8	2.9	33.2
	20.6	21.8	14.1	7.7	64.1

Source: R. Fox (1991).

Table 35. **Training in the European Union**

Per cent of labour force having been trained in a given four-week period

	Total	Exclusively firm	Dual	Exclusively education
Belgium	2.8	1.2	0.3	1.2
Denmark	23.6	9.5	3.1	11.0
Germany	10.1	1.2	4.0	4.9
Greece	1.4	0.5	0.0	0.9
Spain	3.7	0.8	0.0	2.9
France	4.3	1.0	0.7	2.6
Ireland	**7.1**	**4.4**	**0.9**	**1.8**
Italy	2.7	1.2	0.1	1.4
Luxembourg	4.4	2.2	1.2	1.0
Netherlands	24.3	5.8	1.9	16.6
Portugal	5.3	0.6	0.1	4.7
United Kingdom	18.3	5.6	2.7	10.1
EU total	9.3	2.3	1.8	5.2

Source: EU, Labour Force Survey, 1992.

higher education. To some extent, this reflects a difference in education systems as the EU average is raised by high vocational education in the Netherlands, Denmark and Germany. But the responses may also indicate a difference in perception of respondents about the nature of courses being followed in general and higher education.

Ireland has an apprenticeship system covering certain designated trades and which is regulated by the National Training Authority (FAS). Such training combines off-the-job education and vocational training. Apprentices are released from their work either on a daily or monthly basis in order to study in vocational schools, technical colleges or government training centres. Such courses are attended by about 10 000 people each year, representing an annual throughput of around 3 000. A new standards-based apprenticeship system was introduced in September 1993 and will be generalised by September 1995. It will replace the traditional apprenticeship, based on the length of time served, by compulsory standards-based training and education. This new system includes seven phases, three off-the-job and four on-the-job. On successful completion of the standards-based apprenticeship, apprentices will receive a National Craft Certificate that is recognised nationally and internationally. An apprenticeship fund generated through a pay-roll levy of 0.25 per cent and EU aid will provide for training allowances to be paid to the apprentices.

In addition to apprenticeship training, there is a considerable amount of vocational training performed in the education system. Approximately 18 000 people are enrolled in *Post Leaving Certificate* (PLC) courses. The objective of these programmes is to provide vocational training for young people who have completed formal schooling. The schools providing the courses are strongly encouraged to adjust their programmes to the needs of the local labour market. In addition to providing specific vocational training programmes, students in PLCs continue to develop their general education. Since 1991, the National Council for Vocational Awards (NCVA) has had responsibility for the certification and assessment of second-level vocational programmes offered by the PLC courses. There are also a large number of training activities in the higher education sector, especially at the technician level.

Public active labour market policies

Scope

In Ireland, as in other OECD countries, labour market policy has been increasingly focused on more active measures aimed at mobilising labour supply, enhancing employment-related skills and strengthening the efficiency of labour markets. Irish active labour market policies use all the elements found elsewhere: job creation, subsidised employment, youth programmes and training. They have benefited from the financial support of the Community Support Framework (CSF) of the European Union. During the 1990s, some 30 000 people per year have passed through these programmes.

Such active labour-market policies are aimed at early school-leavers, the long-term unemployed and improving the skills of the unemployed. The Department of Education and FAS administer programmes[61] to provide foundation training for about 6 000 young people with poor educational qualifications. For the long-term unemployed, the major training programme is the Vocational Training Opportunities Scheme (VTOS), which is designed to give the long-term unemployed a second chance to obtain leaving certificates. There are several programmes aimed at meeting particular skill demands in local labour markets through training the unemployed. The largest one is the Specific Skills Training Programme (SST) which involves the training of over 14 000 persons annually. Courses are linked directly to the local labour market through instructors who monitor skill needs and conduct placement surveys on completion of each course. For a course to continue, more than 65 per cent of the trainees have to find relevant jobs.

In addition, there are training programmes for those already at work, co-financed by the CSF. The most important are Training Grants, administered by the Industrial Development Agency, which subsidise the induction training of new employees; the Industrial Restructuring Programme, which provides grant aid for companies to purchase training for their employees; the Management Development Programme, which provides training for 400 managers every year; and the Middle Level Training Programme, which supports part-time and short-cycle training in regional technical colleges.

The Department of Education provides more than three-quarters of the overall cost of the public sector vocational training effort while FAS provides the remainder. The bulk of the provision of training resources is financed by the Education Department (Table 36). Even for apprenticeship programmes which it administers, FAS provides less than half of the training resources. The bulk of the training effort is aimed at those who have left school and takes place before they enter the labour market. Training for the unemployed represents about one-fifth of total expenditure. These FAS programmes are relatively expensive as they always entail the payment of training allowances, while the training provided by

Table 36.   **The vocational training effort**

	Numbers trained	Training costs	Allow-ances	Total	Numbers trained	Trained costs	Allow-ances
		Ir£ million			Per cent of total		
Department of Education							
General							
Post-school programmes	32 400	74.7	0.0	74.7	35.7	27.4	0.0
Mid-level technical	16 303	49.3	14.3	63.6	18.0	18.1	19.5
High-level technical	9 021	30.2	7.8	38.0	9.9	11.1	10.6
Advanced technical	2 384	16.4	0.0	16.4	2.6	6.0	0.0
Apprentices	9 518	15.0	0.0	15.0	10.5	5.5	0.0
CERT	2 119	6.5	0.0	6.5	2.3	2.4	0.0
Unemployed							
Second chance education	2 453	7.5	7.0	14.4	2.7	2.7	9.5
Youthreach	1 461	7.5	0.0	7.5	1.6	2.8	0.0
Total of above	75 659	207.1	29.1	236.1	83.4	76.0	39.7
National Training Authority (FAS)							
General							
Apprentices	1 568	11.0	3.2	14.2	1.7	4.0	4.4
Post-school programmes	1 442	5.8	4.4	10.2	1.6	2.1	6.0
Unemployed							
School leavers programmes	4 709	19.0	14.4	33.4	5.2	7.0	19.6
Skill training	5 701	23.0	17.4	40.4	6.3	8.5	23.7
Other programmes	1 596	6.4	4.9	11.3	1.8	2.4	6.6
Total of above	15 016	65.3	44.2	109.5	16.6	24.0	60.3
Education and training	90 675	272.4	73.3	345.6	100.0	100.0	100.0
Memorandum item:							
Community employment schemes							
Community employment	27 631	111.6	84.2	195.8			
Public employment service	0	0.0	0.0	0.0			
Total active labour market measures		383.9	157.5	541.4			

Source: Departments of Education, Employment, Enterprise and Finance.

the Department of Education can generally fill its courses without the payment of allowances. As a result, over 40 per cent of the FAS training budget for the unemployed is devoted to the payment of allowances as opposed to only 15 per cent of the Education budget. In addition to the training programmes, FAS also runs community employment schemes which have some training content.[62] The overall cost of active labour market policies is high, amounting to about 1.3 per cent of GNP and is only surpassed by the size of the Swedish programme while Denmark, Finland and Germany spend similar amounts. The government devotes an additional 1 per cent of GNP on vocational education and training, about half of this is already included in the education budget, with a further $1/4$ per cent of GNP going to allowances.

There is evidence that the return from state-run training programmes for the unemployed in Ireland, as elsewhere, is not very high. The effectiveness of such programmes is usually measured by the success of the participants in finding jobs at the end of their training. Many participants would have presumably found jobs even if they had not received training. To judge the effectiveness of these programmes it is necessary to compare the success of participants in finding a job to that of similar unemployed persons who did not receive training. Ideally, there should also be a comparison of the earnings of the two groups. In 1991, about 70 per cent of the unemployed who took part in the SST programme found jobs in the six months following the completion of their training. On the other hand, it did not appear that participating in training programmes improved the chances of a young person finding a job in the long run compared with the experience of similar unemployed non-participants.[63]

These results for Ireland are similar to those in other countries. The few studies that have been undertaken find little evidence that such programmes are effective.[64] Some surveys have underlined that the programmes for the early school-leavers, as for the long-term unemployed, are not sufficiently integrated with the rest of the education and training system.[65] Since most people in these categories suffer from severe educational disadvantages and low short-term employability, they are likely to experience persistent difficulties in the labour market if the initial programme is not followed by further education, training, guidance and counselling. Post-school training for unqualified school-leavers does not seem to be the most efficient way of increasing their human capital which, rather, requires assistance before leaving school.[66] Indeed, research in other countries suggests that there is a strong correlation between the return from training and education;[67] the higher the level of education, the greater the return from training. For persons with only eight years or less of education, there is little return from training.

Apprenticeships have been one method of providing training in certain skills. In Ireland, the emphasis of past apprenticeship programmes has been on learning-by-doing during a certain period of time. At the end of the period, the apprentice was deemed to be qualified. However, one study of the returns to education in Ireland found that participation in such a training programme generated little economic return.[68] If a person had successfully completed an apprenticeship, his earnings were no higher than those of other workers with a similar level of education and work experience.

Three major problems affect public support of training. First, since most of the support for employee training takes the form of grant aid, there is a possibility that firms would have financed the training courses, at their own expense, in the absence of such aid. Secondly, enterprise-based continued training mainly benefits employees who already have a high level of human capital. Consequently, this form of assistance should not be considered as a means of compensating for an initially inadequate level of education and training. Finally, there is little evidence that training and employment programmes for the unemployed result in an improvement in the economic situation of participants.

Reform proposals

Challenges facing Irish education and training

From the above discussion it appears that there are two principal challenges facing the Irish education system in the next decade: i) how to improve the quality of the education system which, especially for pupils at the lower end of the ability scale, is not up to international standards, thus resulting in a high risk of long-term unemployment for young people who leave school with few or no qualifications; and ii) how to increase the output of the system in order to strengthen economic growth in the face of a fall in the birth rate. Quality improvement seems mainly to be a problem at the primary and junior secondary level, as shown by international comparisons, whereas Irish secondary school leavers appear to be able to compete for higher education places abroad, suggesting that quality is good. Nevertheless, there is evidence that average quality is not completely homogenous as both the performance of children from poorer backgrounds and results of different schools vary considerably. Increasing the output of the educational system over the next five years would be possible through policies aiming to raise the participation rates at secondary schools by adjusting the curriculum options to the broader spectrum of abilities. In addition, a particular effort will be needed to improve the access of lower-status families to education, particularly to third-level studies. Efforts to improve quality and increase output should create the conditions for sustained growth that would allow Ireland to catch up with income levels of the rest of Europe. In addition, this would reduce the numbers of children who leave school without completing the junior secondary cycle and are at a very high risk of long-term unemployment.

The planned changes

In 1992, the government published a discussion paper on the future of education in Ireland.[69] This document contained a large number of proposals for reform, some of which were new, while others had already been suggested. These proposals were discussed at the National Education Convention in October 1993. The Convention promoted mutual understanding among the various partners in education, thereby creating a good foundation on which to continue reforms. Many of the changes proposed in the area of the curriculum have been promulgated but a considerable number of changes have still to be implemented. This section presents some of the reforms proposed in the discussion paper, focusing on those that are relevant to the key problems outlined above.

Qualitative improvements in schools

The major aim of the proposed reforms is to improve the quality of primary and secondary schools and to ensure that as many as possible are able to receive an education that is adapted to their needs. At the *primary level,* this is to be accomplished by improving teaching methods and the content of the curriculum in an attempt to lower the number of children who transfer to secondary schools without basic skills. The reforms will require the teacher to take a more active role in the learning process. While the curriculum will continue to be integrated, it will be divided into more discrete subjects at the older age levels in the primary school. A science course will be recommended to complement the existing environment and nature study programme and national targets for mathematical achievement will be established. The possibility of introducing a programme to increase awareness of continental Europe, perhaps including the study of another European language, will also be studied. Finally, it had proposed instituting national tests at age 7 and 11, with the aggregated results available to the Department of Education for planning purposes and to act as quality control. However, as the result of subsequent discussions, it is likely that a different form of national testing will be adopted.

Another objective of the reforms at the primary level is to deal with the problem of low achievement amongst some pupils, especially those in disadvantaged primary schools. Two main programmes are being implemented. The first is to improve the link between parents and the school by using liaison teachers to involve the parents with the education of their children. The second programme is to use part of the demographic bonus resulting from falling primary school rolls to increase the number of teachers devoted to remedial teaching in primary schools. In addition, the government intends to extend pre-primary school education in disadvantaged areas. This will be aimed mainly at three and four year-olds as most five year-olds are already in primary schools, even though the standard starting age is six years-old. The proportion of Irish children in pre-school education is low compared with other OECD countries (Table 37).

The primary emphasis of the reforms at the *junior secondary level* is to strengthen quality and ensure a more homogenous level of teaching across schools. Curriculum reform in the junior cycle started in 1989 and is now entering a second phase which should provide courses suited to all levels of ability and aptitude. The junior cycle in Ireland is relatively unusual in that it ends with a national externally-assessed examination (the Junior Certificate) at age 15. Although 87 per cent of children transfer to the senior cycle, the examination is being retained to assess students' performance in the national junior cycle curriculum.[70] It was proposed that the legal school-leaving age be raised to 16, so that those with learning difficulties who stay an extra year in the primary school will be obliged to complete the junior cycle.[71]

Quality may also be improved by the reforms proposed in this area with the view to devolving more decision making and control to the individual school.

Table 37. **Pre-school education**

Full time equivalents, 1991
Percentage of age group

	Age			
	2	3	4	5
Canada	..	..	24.1	35.1
United States	..	32.7	56.7	90.2
Japan	..	20.5	57.8	65.1
New Zealand	35.0	71.6	92.6	3.7
Belgium	22.3	96.5	99.4	97.7
Denmark	..	..	..	4.0
France	35.2	98.0	101.3	99.2
Germany	9.2	35.1	70.6	84.1
Ireland	..	**1.3**	**55.3**	**97.6**
Netherlands	..	..	98.3	98.9
Portugal	..	28.2	44.0	63.0
Spain	5.7	27.6	93.5	100.3
United Kingdom	..	44.0	60.7	100.0
Austria	1.0	29.5	65.7	85.4
Norway	19.7	40.0	53.5	61.4
Switzerland	2.0	5.5	26.4	75.8
Turkey	..	..	0.3	1.7
Average of all above countries	7.7	31.2	58.8	68.4
Average where such education exists	16.3	40.8	62.5	68.4

Source: OECD.

Lowering the degree of centralisation in decision making will allow the Department of Education to focus entirely on strategic issues. The proposed reforms envisage a new method for appointing school boards of management which would increase the representation of the parents and teachers, with a corresponding decline in that of the owner or ''patron'' of the school which, in most cases, is a church or religious order.[72] It was proposed that the owner would nominate the chairman of the board but would no longer have a voting majority on it. The board would also be responsible for spending the non-salary budget of the school, which would be allocated to the school on a per capita basis. However, the number of full-time equivalent teachers allocated to the school would still be decided centrally. Various specialised services would be provided to the school by a newly created intermediate authority, which will be responsible for co-ordinating all educational services, including the rationalisation of school facilities.

The board of management would be responsible for the quality of education and teaching in the school – a major change from the current situation where Department of Education inspectors check on the work of each teacher. The role of the inspectors would change to monitoring schools' quality and advising them.[73] More responsibility would be given to the head teacher who, as the "instructional leader", would, with the board become responsible for the hiring and appraising of teachers working in the school. The board of management would have to set out its objectives in an educational plan. The devolution of power would require more local accountability for the results obtained by the school as reflected in tests at the primary level and examination outcome at the secondary level.

Increasing participation rates

Reform of the curriculum in the *senior secondary cycle* is aimed at improving the participation rate by offering courses to students of below average ability. The existing structure of the cycle is essentially based on a curriculum designed for the upper half of the ability range who are capable of proceeding to tertiary education. The mismatch between these courses and the expectations of lower-ability students has provoked a certain degree of dissatisfaction,[74] which may grow as the senior cycle expands.

A threefold reform is envisaged. First, since 1994 pupils have had the option of adding another year at the start of the senior cycle, making the programme last three years. As a transition year, it is intended to help students identify their strengths and weaknesses and develop basic competencies using, if necessary, remedial education. It will not be an opportunity for spreading the two-year LC course over three years. Also, in order to provide courses more adapted to the full range of abilities, a new "applied" level is being added to the Leaving Certificate. This new level will function as an entry qualification to vocational training and education but will not be accepted for immediate entry to third-level education. Finally, a new vocational course will be introduced as part of the general LC level. It will differ from other LC courses in that about 6 per cent of the teaching time will be allocated to modules which provide a linkage to the world outside the school, notably through the acquisition of communication and other personal skills and through case studies of local enterprises and work experience. In addition, two of the six standard courses must have a practical orientation.

The principal proposals for the tertiary sector were to allow the proportion of the age group entering higher education to rise to 45 per cent over the medium term. As to the content of the courses offered, the government felt that it was necessary to avoid academic drift in the sub-degree courses by keeping them as applied as possible. It also announced a review of grant policy for students with the objective of removing outstanding anomalies or barriers which may hinder the participation of children from disadvantaged backgrounds.

The focus on training

The government has proposed that there should be a consolidation of the vocational training effort so that the system becomes more cohesive with the acquisition of qualifications occurring in a graduated and modularised form. The basis for this consolidation will be a new system for the certification and accreditation of competencies and knowledge acquired during training. The eventual objective is to provide theoretical training and general education in schools, while practical training will be given by employers. The speed with which such a system will be introduced, though, will depend on the extent of co-operation by employers. The National Education and Training Certification Board intends to develop a comprehensive system of national certification and validation of standards in secondary and non-university tertiary education as well as vocational training programmes, thus co-ordinating the work of existing bodies.

Global assessment and scope for further action

As noted, the proposed changes in the curriculum and teaching methods at the primary level should improve the quality of education. At the same time, the resources available for disadvantaged schools may, to some extent, already have been preempted as nearly two-thirds of the demographic "dividend" has been spent with the generalised reduction in the pupil-teacher ratio (Diagram 20). Such a sharp increase in expenditure per pupil should result in higher quality output, but it will be essential to monitor results; in this context, it is of concern that there is no plan to publish the results of national testing which may be introduced at the primary school level. It is less clear whether the proposals for significant increases in non-teaching staff at the secondary level will improve quality, so spending large amounts on administration does not seem justified.

The decentralisation of decision making to a local level may also result in improvements in performance. The proposals to give more managerial power to the head teacher, who will be responsible for the quality of the education provided, may improve results since most research stresses the role of good leadership in raising standards.[75] However, the new duties of head teachers will represent a marked change in their responsibilities and a training programme may be required to facilitate the transition. The prevalence of small schools may be one of the reasons that the distribution of performance across schools is much more uneven in Ireland than in other countries. It was suggested that considerable rationalisation of schools will be needed, an orientation supported by the National Education Convention. Indeed, the convention proposed an essentially political process for deciding on school closure rather than accepting the role of what it called "destructive" competition. At the senior secondary level, the reform proposals go a long way to offering a range of options that should make general education more attractive to the much wider spectrum of ability levels that are now entering this cycle. The option given to pupils to extend the senior cycle to three years should also help lower ability ranges to establish sound bases for progression in the senior cycle. The decision to offer vocational education after the completion of secondary education, rather than as a separate stream of secondary education, also seems to fit with the tendency to place value on general education, though it goes against calls by earlier government studies such as the "Culliton Report" for the creation of a separate vocational education stream in the secondary cycle.

Another possible method to improve quality would be to increase the public pressure on schools to perform well by publishing the results of standardised tests on a school-by-school basis. This would make schools directly accountable to the communities they serve for their performance. The introduction of national testing at ages 7 and 11 with publication of results would be beneficial. The results of the national assessment might be used on a school-by-school basis to identify the poorly-performing institutions so that they could be reorganised and allocated additional resources if necessary. Rather than accept poor results supposedly associated with the social background of parents, such an approach would enable the education system to overcome these handicaps.

Finally, quality could also be improved by lengthening the school year, bringing it into line with the OECD average. Such a policy would ease the heavy burden that is placed on the primary curriculum and would allow for more structured in-career development for teachers, so increasing the weight given to science and mathematics without reducing the time spent on the Irish language and religion. Such a change might also allow the introduction of a continental European language. Despite the proposed reforms, the allocation of time to science and mathematics in the junior secondary cycle will remain low by international standards[76] while technology will cease to be a core subject from 1996, so reducing the incentive for the more academic schools to offer good courses in the subject.

The principal proposals for increasing participation in education come at the tertiary level, but here the question arises as to whether such an expansion would be worthwhile, in economic terms, given that a large number of Irish graduates emigrate. A priori, a large outflow of graduates does not necessarily make expansion uneconomic, and indeed social returns appear high even allowing for the cost of migration. Another objection to expansion in higher education is that the additional need in this area may be only temporary given that the size of the age group will start to fall in five to ten years. In this regard, it must be stressed, however, that there is strong upward movement in participation rates which may well continue beyond the end of the decade, partly offsetting demographic movements. As the shortfall in skills appears to be at a level between secondary school and universities, it will be necessary to ensure that the eventual expansion of higher education is concentrated on the sub-degree sector. Of course, care should be taken in designing teaching at this level to ensure that it offers the possibility for advancement to degree-level education, allowing students to progress. Such advancement opportunities are all the more important given that children from lower-status backgrounds are more likely to be found at this level than at universities.

The proposals to reduce the charges for education should be assessed in light of whether they are likely to lead to higher participation rates. In higher education, the decision in the 1995 Budget to abolish fees and increase grants for middle and high-income families are unlikely to raise participation since the children from these backgrounds already have high participation rates. On the other hand, students from low-income backgrounds may have been deterred by the existence of fees even though they would have benefited from a means-tested government grant which would pay their fees and so participation rates in these groups could rise. The decision to extend maintenance grants to those who study abroad may encourage emigration. The benefit of using foreign educational facilities would be lost if, as is perhaps likely, the graduates did not return. However, more carefully targeted use of higher education grants for children from low-income families, might raise participation in education and might, therefore, be worth considering.

In the training sector, efforts to modernise apprenticeship appear to have worked well, with the qualification obtained being recognised internationally. The new National Education and Training Certification Board will determine standards and co-ordinate the awards given by the various training agencies. It would be desirable to ensure that there are clear paths available for students to be able to advance from one level to another.

Although some of the curriculum reforms are now beginning to be implemented in schools, there remain a number of important decisions to be finalised. In the course of public discussion at the National Education Convention, a wide range of proposals were canvassed. One rough estimate put the cost of all the proposed changes at 2 per cent of GNP or 30 per cent of the education budget. The magnitude of this cost indicates a clear need to evaluate and prioritise both within the education budget and government expenditure in general, as such an increase in expenditure would conflict with the need to restrain overall government expenditure.

The most important priorities for progress in reforming education and training seem to be in the following areas:
-   improvement in the quality of education in schools, especially at the primary level, by increasing resources for disadvantaged schools and pupils;
-   lengthening the school year in order to give greater weight to mathematics, science and foreign languages at the primary school level, together with increased in-service training in these areas;
-   reducing the financial costs of tertiary education for the children of low-income families through better targeting of existing expenditure;
-   expanding the tertiary sector, especially at the sub-degree level.

The education budget has the scope to self-finance some priority reforms through the expected demographic ''dividend'' over the next six years, provided class sizes are kept constant. Any further increases in expenditure will need to proceed very gradually unless there is a reasignment of priorities within overall government spending.

V. Conclusions

The Irish economy has achieved the fastest growth in the European Union over the past three years. Output increased by almost 4 per cent in 1993, when the rest of Europe fell into recession, and by a further 5½ per cent in 1994. The expansion in activity was led by exports from the modern manufacturing sector, which offset depressed conditions in the domestic market in the first half of 1993. A second ingredient to growth was the removal, following the 10 per cent devaluation of the currency within the EMS in January 1993, of exchange and interest rate pressures associated with the disruption of European exchange markets in the autumn of 1992. This allowed a rapid easing in monetary conditions which boosted household and business confidence, thus facilitating a recovery of domestic demand in the second half of 1993, led by consumption and increased investment in housing. As a result, the unemployment rate declined significantly in 1994, although – at 14½ per cent – it still represents the third highest in the OECD area. At the same time, inflation stabilised at about 2½ per cent, aided by continued wage moderation and a gradual appreciation of the currency which, by the end of 1994, brought the effective exchange rate to only 1 per cent below its level in the summer of 1992.

The economic outlook for 1995 and 1996 remains favourable with output growth projected to be near 5 per cent. Continued growth in employment and real disposable income should sustain personal consumption, although higher interest rates may slow the growth of housebuilding. Activity will also benefit from increased exports, led by demand for traditional products from continental Europe. With the upturn becoming more established and broad-based, business investment in structures and buildings, which has a high domestic content, should increase, thereby strengthening activity. The expected growth should be sufficient to ensure a further reduction in unemployment. Although inflation is currently under control, the continuing decline in the number of jobless might put upward pressure on wage rates, and consequently on domestic prices, the more so since a further improvement in the UK labour market could encourage the emigration of Irish workers. Such developments could first emerge in sheltered areas of the economy, especially in the construction sector where demand is strong and credit has been expanding rapidly.

Interest rate developments over the past two years suggest that monetary policy has helped establish confidence of the markets in the stability of the new central rate of the Irish pound. With the marked fall of money market rates from a peak of over 40 per cent at the beginning of 1993 to just over 6 per cent at the end of 1994, the differential between German and Irish short-term interest rates has come back to the level prior to the currency market disturbances of the autumn of 1992. Likewise, by the end of 1994 the differential between Irish and German long-term rates had fallen to below the level observed in the middle of 1992. However, Irish long-term interest rates remained more in line with UK rates, rising faster than German rates in early 1994 before stabilising in the second half of the year despite further upward pressure in Germany.

As the economic cycle in Ireland is further advanced than in continental Europe, being closer to that in the United Kingdom, the need to tighten monetary conditions, in order to avoid a buildup of inflationary tensions, is arising earlier there than in other ERM countries. Consequently, the rise in short-term interest rates in March 1995, in the context of a generalised weakness of European currencies against the Deutschemark, would seem to be appropriate on domestic grounds as well as for exchange-rate reasons. While such a preventive action should help strengthen confidence in the authorities commitment to price stability, domestic inflationary pressure will have to be carefully weighed when implementing monetary policy in the period ahead. In so doing, the task of the monetary authorities should be facilitated by the wider bands which have been in operation within the European Exchange Rate Mechanism since August 1993.

Given the rapid easing of monetary conditions from the beginning of 1993, there was much less pressure in Ireland than elsewhere in Europe to use fiscal policy to support growth. The budget position has remained under control, with actual deficits in 1993 and 1994 (at 2¼ per cent of GDP) lower than initially envisaged. This favourable outcome resulted mainly from the additional tax revenue generated by the faster-than-expected economic growth. A major part of this "tax bonus" has been used to expand public expenditure. Overall, government spending (excluding debt service) rose by 17 per cent over the last two years, despite an increase in the price level of only 4 per cent. In an attempt to curb this trend, the new government announced its intention to limit the growth of nominal expenditure to 6 per cent during 1995 and 2 per cent above inflation in each of the subsequent two years. Nevertheless, the budget deficit is officially projected to rise in 1995 to 2¾ per cent of GDP which, given the continuation of rapid economic growth, suggests a somewhat pro-cyclical stance of fiscal policy.

With government borrowing remaining low, the debt-to-GDP ratio is projected to fall to 85 per cent by the end of 1995 from 97 per cent in 1990, despite the increase in the value of the foreign currency portion of the debt due to the devaluation. During the current period of rapid growth and buoyant tax revenues, a sustained rundown of debt would be appropriate, in order to reduce the risk premia built into the persistently high level of long-term real interest rates. To achieve this, it would be essential to slow down the increase in government expenditure to well below the growth rate of national income. While current expenditure targets are consistent with reducing the debt ratio towards 60 per cent by the end of the century, as required by the Maastricht Treaty, the credibility of fiscal policy would benefit from the formulation of a more detailed medium-term fiscal strategy taking into account the need to save rather than spend cyclical gains in tax revenue.

One factor responsible for the pressure on public spending has been the incomes policies in operation since 1988, in the form of three-year programmes including a centralised wage agreement between the social partners. The current *Programme for Competitiveness and Work* (PCW), which covers the years 1994-96, envisages limiting wage increases to about 8 per cent in total during that period, in line with the expected rate of inflation. In exchange for wage moderation, however, the PCW commits the government to boost social welfare spending and to reduce the tax burden on workers within the limits of the authorities' fiscal goals. While this type of agreement proved to be successful in limiting inflationary pressure and promoting social cohesion, notably after the devaluation of early 1993, it constitutes also a constraint for fiscal policy which could, in the long run, undermine the priority attached to reducing public debt. More importantly, by reducing the responsiveness of wages to shifts in the relative demand for labour, the centrally-determined pay increases implied by such agreements may tend to introduce further rigidities into the labour market.

The rate of long-term unemployment in Ireland – the highest in the OECD area – is indeed partly related to the lack of incentives for the unemployed (particularly young people with a low level of education) to take low-paid employment. This is due to the flat-rate nature of unemployment benefits and the large gap between child benefits paid to the unemployed and those paid to the employed. The problem has been aggravated over the past decade as unemployment benefits increased faster than take-home pay. In the 1994 Budget, the government reformed the unemployment insurance system by abolishing the earnings-related supplement that was previously payable during the first year of unemployment, and by making benefits taxable. This orientation was continued in the 1995 Budget by keeping unemployment benefits in line with prices while reducing taxes on the low paid. In addition, to increase work incentives for the unemployed with families, the relative gap between the child benefits paid to the unemployed and to those who are working was narrowed. Although these measures lowered the "replacement rates" (the ratio of income when unemployed to take-home pay) reducing long-term unemployment would require further significant reforms. In particular, a better administration of benefits would be needed to ensure that unemployed people are looking for work. In view of the concentration of unemployment amongst the young, consideration should also be given to allowing the full rate of unemployment payments only to adults with a substantial record of participation in the labour force. Reforms in other areas, such as the abolition of minimum wage agreements in order to increase the supply of low-paid jobs, might be needed as well. Finally, over the longer term, improving the education of the young should make for a more successful transition from school to work, minimising the risk of unemployment.

Education in Ireland, the subject of this Survey's special chapter, has improved significantly over the past generation: the provision of free secondary education has boosted previously low participation rates to a level slightly above the OECD average; the expansion of higher education has made Ireland second only to Japan in the proportion of young workers with a scientific or engineering degree; and although the average educational qualification of the labour force is still low, it will rise rapidly as youths currently in school enter the labour force. Despite a much higher number of pupils relative to the working population, public expenditure on education is not much above the OECD average, indicating an efficient use of the resources devoted to that sector. Also, quality has been kept relatively high partly because spending has been concentrated on teachers, rather than on support staff and materials. Nevertheless, the Irish education system still lags behind that of the most advanced countries in some respects. Almost one-quarter of students do not complete a full secondary education and there are certain subject areas, such as science, where quality and achievement are low at the beginning of the secondary cycle. In addition, educational performance in Ireland is more variable across primary schools than in other OECD countries, so that a considerable minority of children enter secondary schools without necessary skills. As a result, children from lower socio-economic backgrounds are almost five times as likely to leave school with low qualifications and face a 50 per cent probability of being unemployed one year after leaving school.

Resolving these weaknesses of the education system would help Ireland to boost productivity and income to levels comparable to those in continental Europe. At the same time, this would contribute to reducing the high proportion of long-term unemployment among the young if accompanied by increased labour market flexibility. The government has already planned reforms to improve the quality of education at the primary and secondary levels. A new science course will be introduced at the primary level and teaching methods will be changed to have more specific learning objectives at each stage. At the secondary level, the junior cycle will have a core curriculum to ensure the acquisition of basic skills. Additional courses are being implemented at the senior level to better match a broad range of ability. A supplementary, but optional, year is also being added to the senior secondary cycle, bringing the standard age at which the secondary cycle is completed up to 18, in line with that in most other OECD countries.

While such steps should go a considerable way towards lowering the number of school-leavers with low qualifications, other options currently debated would need to be pursued such as concentrating the resources made available by the fall in the birth rate on poorly-performing schools and children rather than using them to reduce class sizes on a generalised basis. The return to society could be high in this area, since it might result in an eventual fall in long-term unemployment. Given the small size of many Irish schools, such action may require class and school closures, which should be based on performance-related criteria. In this context, and given the greater planned decentralisation of decision-making to schools, there is a need for national assessment at certain critical periods, such as age 8, and before transfer to secondary schools. Transparency in this field could increase pressure for schools to improve their performance. One further method of improving quality might be to increase the time spent on core subjects, such as science and mathematics, by progressively lengthening the Irish school year, currently one of the shortest in the OECD area.

With respect to tertiary education, the problem arises as to whether the government should increase the capacity of existing universities and technical colleges to respond to rising demand in that area. The economic returns to higher education are such that its expansion would be justified to improve human capital. Indeed, graduates would presumably have relatively less problem finding employment either in Ireland or abroad. Although demographic developments would tend to reduce the number of students going to university from the beginning of the next century, thus arguing for caution in expanding this sector, this trend could be offset by the increasing proportion of school leavers entering higher education, as well as by a lengthening of courses in this field and by entry of adults into higher education.

The level of human capital also depends on the amount of training provided. The training effort in Ireland has resulted in a skill profile of the labour force that is similar to other countries, except at intermediate levels of education (*i.e.* between the secondary and university levels), where it appears to be deficient. Although this deficiency is partially offset by a higher level of on-job training in firms than is found in other European countries, the National Training Agency has undertaken a major overhaul of craft training in a number of skills. In these occupations, the traditional apprenticeship has been replaced by modular courses based on alternate periods of theoretical instruction in educational or training centres and periods of practical experience in a firm. In addition, the Department of Education is improving the quality of the courses offered at the post-secondary level in schools. Given the diversity of available training programmes, the government would need to ensure that the certification and advancement opportunities are coherent, to offer students the possibility of progressively upgrading their qualifications through the educational system and to ensure that credentials are acceptable internationally. It would also be necessary that the organisation chosen to oversee post-secondary vocational education and training have a high reputation, in order to draw the maximum number of educational establishments into its net.

In addition to formal and private training, Ireland has large active labour market programmes, the third biggest in the OECD area in terms of government spending relative to GNP. However, while many participants in such programmes find jobs at the end of the courses, studies suggest that a large number might have found employment in any case. Proposed changes to the largest of the programmes (Community Employment Scheme) would add a series of basic education modules designed to improve the poor educational performance of long-term unemployed youths, for whom these courses are designed. Indeed, an expansion of one of the most successful of the active labour market programmes, which offers the unemployed the possibility to return to the senior cycle of secondary education, might be justified.

Beyond education and training, further reforms to improve the tax system and to promote competition would also have a positive effect on growth. Despite improvement in the 1995 Budget, further reductions in tax rates would improve work incentives. These could be financed through a broadening of the tax base in order to ensure revenue neutrality. While the tax deductibility of mortgage interest payments and certain private-income transfers are being reduced, a wider tax base could be achieved by reducing the scale of schemes designed to favour investment in certain enterprises, which have proved costly for public finances. In the area of competition, the establishment of a new Authority in 1991 has focused attention on preventing anti-competitive practices. The reforms recently proposed by the government to grant extra resources and stronger enforcement powers, thus allowing the Authority greater freedom to initiate actions, are intended to promote this objective.

In summary, the Irish economy appears set to continue its recent rapid growth based on the recovery of domestic demand and buoyant exports. Inflation has remained subdued, aided by continued wage moderation and a monetary policy geared towards maintaining exchange rate stability. With employment growing rapidly, there is a possibility that upward pressure on wages could develop despite current income policies. Monetary policy must remain focused on preventing an acceleration of inflation. In addition, policy makers remain confronted with the necessity to reduce the still high public debt and unemployment levels. Although the faster-than-expected growth in tax revenues has considerably improved the public finance position, continued progress in lowering the debt-to-GDP ratio in line with the Maastricht criteria, while making room for further reduction in the tax burden, would require tighter control on public expenditure. Reducing unemployment would call for reforms to further increase the incentives to work and improve the flexibility of the labour market. Improvement of the education system would also help over time to lower the high proportion of long-term unemployed. By strengthening and broadening growth, such reforms would further narrow the gap between living standards in Ireland and the more advanced OECD countries.

Notes

1. The introduction of the Intrastat system at the beginning of 1993 has made statistics for trade within the EU less precise. As a result, the figures for 1993 are not fully comparable with 1992.

2. The rise in profit repatriation in 1993 slowed GNP growth to 3.6 per cent compared to 4 per cent for GDP. Profit repatriation accounted for 12 per cent of GNP in that year.

3. Materials used for further processing accounted for 57 per cent of imports in 1993.

4. In recent years, export prices have declined mainly because of the falling prices of computers, an important component of Irish exports.

5. Net fiscally-related external transfers declined from 3.2 per cent of GNP in 1991 to 2.6 per cent 1993. This is due to a fall in current transfers from the EU from 7.3 per cent of GNP to 6.2 per cent over the same period.

6. The PESP provided for pay increases of 4 per cent in 1991, 3 per cent in 1992 and 3.75 per cent in 1993. Including the 3 per cent that could be negotiated at the local level, wages at the end of 1993 could have been up to 14.5 per cent higher than at the end of 1990. While the agreement also covered public service employees, special clauses allowed their wages to rise 24 per cent between 1990 and 1993. Public service employees received deferred payments agreed to under the previous central wage agreement, *Programme for National Recovery,* which was in effect from 1988 to 1990.

7. This rate refers to the standardised unemployment rate.

8. See *OECD Economic Outlook No. 56,* December 1994.

9. The statistics for credit growth overstate the growth in domestic demand for credit due to the growing importance of credit activity in the International Finance and Services Centre (IFSC). In the official statistics, such lending is included in lending to the other financial sector. This lending is generally in foreign currency and is lent mainly to non-banking institutions in the IFSC rather than to non-residents.

10. After allowing for the valuation change in foreign currency debt and lending in the IFSC.

11. This is equivalent to a target of 85 per cent of GDP which is more commonly used as the denominator for debt comparisons across countries.

12. The two areas covered were repaying the borrowing of local health boards and the initial payment towards meeting the liability of the Post Office and Telecom pension fund incurred prior to its separation from the governments' own accounts.

13. Relative to GNP, the gross debt fell by more than 6 points to 102 per cent at the end of 1994, down from a peak of 130 per cent in 1986.

14. Several funds and agencies (notably the National Treasury Management Agency, the Intervention Agency, the Post Office Savings Bank), which are off-budget as far as the EBR is concerned, are included in the central government subsector of the general government account.

15. Both calculations assume a gross employment income of Ir£ 250 per week (equal to the average industrial wage) and maximum entitlement to Pay Related Benefit.

16. The earnings potential of a person with only primary education is 75 per cent of that of a person with average education, while a person aged 20 is subject to a further 33 per cent discount due to his lack of experience compared with the average worker.

17. The exemption of pension fund income is a practice that is common to other OECD countries, such as the United Kingdom.

18. A. Matthews (1994), "Implications of the GATT Uruguay Round Agreement for the Irish economy" in *Economic Perspectives for the Medium-term,* ESRI, Dublin.

19. A detailed examination of these changes in competition policy is given in the 1993 OECD Survey, pp. 69-97.

20. For example, the Authority's decision that two grocery stores could not advertise supposed manufacturers' maximum recommended prices, following the abolition of retail price maintenance, was ignored according to the weekly magazine "Business and Finance" (3 November 1994).

21. A full description of the proposed changes can be found in the Green Paper on Education.

22. The results of the national consultation were published by the Secretariat of the National Convention.

23. In 1990, overseas-owned companies accounted for 94.5 per cent of net output and 78.8 per cent of employment in the high-tech industrial sector.

24. Mankiw, Romer and Weil (1992), "A contribution to the empirics of economic growth", *Quarterly Journal of Economics.*

25. See, for example, Barro (1991), "Economic growth in a cross section of countries", *Quarterly Journal of Economics,* and Levine, Ross and Renelt (1992), "A sensitivity analysis of cross-country growth regressions", *American Economic Review.*

26. This is illustrated in Englander and Gurney (1994), "Medium-term determinants of OECD productivity", *OECD Economic Studies,* No. 22.

27. Surveys of groups of people where the amount of education received was random have found that education does have an impact separate from underlying ability and have confirmed the relationship generally identified between earnings and education. One such study used earnings and education data from a sample of separated identical twins. Its results suggest that it is legitimate to attribute correlation between length of education and earnings differentials to education rather than to inherited variables. See J. Angrist and A. Krueger (1992), "Does compulsory school education affect earnings", *Quarterly Journal of Economics,* CVI, pp. 979 to 1014. Angst and Krueger, "Estimating the payoff to schooling using the Vietnam era draft lottery", *NBER Working Papers,* No. 4067. Aschenfelter and Krueger (1992),

"Estimates of the economic return from schooling from a new sample of twins", *NBER Working Papers*, No. 4143.

28. See "Returns to educational investment", Appendix 3 to the Community support framework, *ESRI and DKB Consultants*, Dublin, 1993 (unpublished). The data was drawn from "Survey of income distribution, poverty and the usage of state services", *Economic and Social Research Institute*, Dublin. See "Poverty, income and welfare in Ireland", T. Callan, B. Nolan *et al.*, *Economic and Social Research Institute, General research paper No. 146*, Dublin (1989), for a description of the survey.

29. The research for Ireland used the level of education rather than the number of years of education as an explanatory variable. To bring the data onto a comparable basis to the results for other countries, it was assumed that the university degree course lasted four years, on average.

30. ESRI and DKB Consultants.

31. The earnings of migrants should be ignored in a calculation of the social rate of return, if the objective of the calculation is to maximise income in Ireland. However, if the objective of society were to maximise the income of Irish people wherever they live, then it would be appropriate to include the income of migrants. Moreover, Ireland is unusual in that one-third of government expenditure on higher education is funded by the European Union and this income flow offsets, to some extent, the loss of emigrants' earnings.

32. In this case, the increase in taxation resulting from the higher earnings of graduates is compared to the cost to the government of providing the education.

33. The Secretariat has assumed that 20 per cent of school and university graduates emigrate, but even if no allowance is made for EU funding and graduate migration rises to 50 per cent, the real rate of return for the government remains as high as 9 per cent. The social rate of return would appears to be somewhat higher than this as some part of emigrants' after tax salary should be counted in the calculation of social returns.

34. See R. Breen and D.F. Hannan, "Returns to education: Irish employers use of educational credentials", *European network on young peoples transitions from education to the labour market*, Conference proceedings Barcelona, Spain (September 1993).

35. See the OECD Jobs Study, Vol. II, "Evidence and Explanations" p. 175, Table 8.1.

36. The Junior Certificate is awarded at the end of the first secondary cycle.

37. Such a group represents a higher proportion of school leavers in the labour force, as many of those with Leaving Certificates do not enter the labour market but pursue further studies.

38. R. Breen and D.F. Hannan, *op. cit.*

39. This draws from the as yet unpublished study by Dr. P. Clancy: "Participation of the socially and economically disadvantaged", University College Dublin and the Higher Education Authority.

40. This group is defined to include the CSO occupational groups professional staff, self-employed, managers, salaried staff and intermediate non-manual occupations.

41. In 1987-88, about 40 per cent of Irish engineering graduates left Ireland to find work abroad. The high rate of emigration may either be due to the relatively small size of Irish firms limiting their ability to offer attractive careers, especially when the high marginal tax rates

are taken into account, or to firms not perceiving the need to employ skilled staff in sufficient numbers.

42. See Roche and Tansey (1992), "Industrial training in Ireland, a study prepared for the Industrial Policy Review group", *Dublin Stationery Office*.

43. See Roche and Tansey, cited above.

44. See O'Farrell and Hitchens (1989), *Small firm competitiveness and performance,* Dublin: Gill and Macmillan.

45. Fahey (1993), "Qualifications and adaptability in labour markets in Ireland", Report for the European Employment Observatory. *Economic and Social Research Institute,* Dublin.

46. NESC, (1993).

47. A fuller description and analysis of the Irish education system is to be found in "Review of National Education Policy: Ireland", OECD (1991).

48. About 2 per cent of primary school age children are enrolled in private schools which receive no state support or supervision. About 7 per cent of secondary schools are fee-charging institutions. Even in the case of these schools, though, the government pays almost all of the teachers' salaries.

49. The proportion of total expenditure which has to be raised locally is lower in poorer areas.

50. About Ir£ 100 million pounds were paid out in 1994 in tuition fees and maintenance grants under various student support schemes including ESF Training grants. Approximately 50 per cent of university students and 90 per cent of technical college students have their fees paid or are in receipt of maintenance grants.

51. This projection is based on current enrolment rates remaining constant for the next 40 years. Human capital is measured by weighting earnings at each education level by the proportion of the population with that level of education, on the assumption that relative earnings stay constant.

52. The results are taken from Lapointe, Mead and Askew, "Learning Mathematics"; "Learning Science" IAEP. Princeton, New Jersey (1992); and Elley "How in the world do students read", IAEEA (1992), The Hague, Netherlands. Diagram 24 shows the results for OECD countries in these reports, as well as non-member countries with comparable levels of per capita income.

53. Some academics dispute the validity of the government tests, however, suggesting that the content of the test has little direct relationship to actual reading activities of the pupils.

54. M. Morgon and M. Martin, *Literacy problems among Irish fourteen year-olds,* Dublin, Educational Research Centre, 1994.

55. The selection of pupils, different home backgrounds and difference in equipment available are other factors influencing the variability of results.

56. D. Card and A. Krueger, "Does school quality matter, returns to education and the characteristics of public schools in the US", *Journal of Political Economy,* 100, pp. 1 to 40.

57. The elasticities with respect to school year, school day and class size were found to be 0.33, –0.19 and –0.15 respectively. The coefficients were significant at about the 10 per cent level. The last correlation between class size and performance only holds, though, if special

allowance is made for the high size of classes in East Asian countries. If this is not taken into account, the relationship between class size and performance become positive.

58. The relatively high pay of teachers attracts students. The academic qualifications of entrants to teacher training colleges are often higher than those of applicants for many degree courses.

59. See Psacharoulos (1993). The lower return on vocational secondary education is largely attributable to its higher cost. Most of the studies were carried out in developing countries which may limit the validity of the conclusions. The same result was found, though, on two studies in Canada and France.

60. See R. Fox (1991), "Total training expenditure in Ireland: initial estimates", *Labour Market Review,* FAS. Fox estimates that total expenditure on formal off-the-job training in the non-agricultural economy, including trainee wage costs, is about 0.9 per cent of labour costs. He also estimates that on-the-job training involves the same level of expenditures.

61. Youth Reach, Community Youth Training Programme, Community Training Workshops and the Skills Foundation Programme.

62. In 1994, a new FAS programme, Community Employment, was launched, targeting on the most disadvantaged amongst the long-term unemployed. Its main objective is to reinforce the links with other training and educational programmes in order to improve the job prospects of the long-term unemployed.

63. Breen, 1991.

64. See OECD *Employment Outlook,* 1993 p. 58.

65. Philip J. O'Connell and J.J. Sexton (1993), "Evaluation of the Operational Programme for the Occupational Integration of young People in Ireland: Objective 4 of the Community Support Framework." ESRI report to the Department of Labour and the European Commission, DG5.

66. Breen, 1991.

67. Psacharopoulos and Velez (1992) "Does training pay independently of Education? Some Evidence from Colombia", *International Journal of Educational Research.*

68. ESRI and DKM Consultants, 1993.

69. "Education for a Changing World", Department of Education (1992).

70. The compulsory subjects to be examined at age 15 are: the Irish language, English, Mathematics, Science and either a combination of History and Geography or Environmental and Social Studies. Students are also examined in optional subjects, such as art, home economics and wood and metal technology.

71. About 30 per cent of children leave primary school one year late, at 13, and so have not completed the junior secondary cycle at age 15.

72. Vocational schools are owned by a local authority committee while one group of schools is owned directly by the Department of Education. The legal ownership of the property rests with the patron who, in most cases, provided the land, though the government paid for the buildings.

73. The Inspectorate, though, will remain responsible for setting, marking and supervising all external examinations, so absorbing much of their resources. An earlier report (OECD, 1991) recommended that this work should be hived off from the Inspectorate.

74. See Hannan and Shortall, "The quality of their education", *ESRI General Paper 153,* 1991.

75. One-third of all primary-school teachers were singled out for criticism in the crucial area of oral-aural English language development in primary schools. See "English in Primary Schools: a survey report", Department of Education curriculum unit, Dublin 1983.

76. The suggested allocation of time to mathematics is 165 minutes per week in contrast to an international average of 213 minutes. For science, schools abroad spend, on average, 188 minutes but the suggested time for technology and science together in Ireland is only 165 minutes.

Bibliography

Breen, R. (1991), "Education, employment and training in the youth labour market", *ESRI Paper 152.*

Breen, R. (1991), "Assessing the effectiveness of training and temporary employment schemes, evidence from the youth labour market", *Economic and Social Review.*

Breen, R. and B. Halpin (1988), "Self employment and unemployment", *ESRI Paper 140.*

Breen, R. and D.F. Hannan (1993), "Returns to education: Irish employers use of educational credentials" in the European Network Conference on young peoples' transition from education to the labour market, Barcelona.

Breen and Shortall (1992), "The exchequer costs of unemployment amongst unqualified labour market participants in the role of the structural funds", *Economic and Social Research Institute Policy Research Paper 13.*

Callan, T. (1992), "Who benefits from public expenditure on education?", *Working Paper 32.*

Callan, T., Nolan and Whelan (1989), "Poverty income and welfare in Ireland", *Economic Social Research Institute Research Paper 146.*

Callan, T., and B. Reilly (1993), "Unions and the wage distribution", *The Economic and Social Review,* July.

CERI (1992), "Adult illiteracy and economic performance", OECD.

Clancy, P., "Participation of the socially and economically disadvantaged", Higher Education Authority.

Clotfelter, C.T., R.G. Ehrengerg, J.J. Siegfried (1991), "Economic challenges in higher education", NBER University of Chicago Press.

Competition Authority (1991), (1992), (1993), Annual reports.

Coolahan, J., "The System of Education in the Republic of Ireland", *The International Encyclopedia of Education.*

Coolahan, J. (1993), "Human resources in the universities of a changing Europe. Regional implications: the Irish university perspective", CRE Conference.

Coolahan, J., "Secondary Education in Ireland", in *Secondary Education for Europe,* (The Council for Secondary Education).

Corcoran, T. and S. Sexton, "An analysis of occupational and change in the industrial and service sectors 1971-1996", in *Employment Observatory* (Commission of the European Communities).

Culliton (1992), *A time for change Industrial policy for the 1990s,* (a report of the Industrial Policy Review Group).

Department of Education (1990), *Report of the Special Education Review Body.*

Department of Education (1991/92), *Statistical Report.*

Department of Education (1992), *Education for a changing world, Green Paper.*

Department of Education (1992), *Preparing for the new Europe. A national framework for vocational qualifications.*

Department of Education (1993), *Presentation to the National Education Convention.*

Department of Education (1993), *The leaving certificate vocational programme.*

Department of Education (1993), *Transition year programmes.*

Department of Education (1993), *Report of the Special Education Committee.*

Department of Education (1994), *Report on round table discussions on the government's position paper on regional education councils.*

Department of Education (1994), *Position paper on the governance of schools.*

Department of Education (1994), *Position paper on Regional Education Councils.*

Department of Education, *Revised structure and content of Senior cycle curriculum 1995 and onwards,* (Circular M47/93).

Department of Enterprise and Employment (1993), *Economic Status of School leavers, 1991.*

Department of Industry and Commerce (1990), *Review of industrial performance.*

Elbaum, "The persistence of apprenticeships in the United Kingdom and its decline in the United States" in H. Gospel, *Industrial training and technological innovation,* Routledge.

Elley, W.B., "How in the world do students read: IEA study of reading literacy", International Association for Evaluation of Educational Achievement.

ESRI (1992), *The role of structural funds in Ireland consequences in the context of 1992.*

ESRI (1994), *Basic income schemes for Ireland.*

ESRI and DKM associates, "Returns to educational investment: new evidence for Ireland".

European Commission (1994), *Ireland Community Support Framework, 1994-99.*

Fahey, T., "Qualifications and adaptability in the labour market", Economic and Social Research Institute.

Fitz Gerald, J. (1994), *Medium term review 1994-2000,* (April).

Fitz Gerald, J. (1994), "Babies, budgets and bathwater", Economic and Social Research Institute, (November).

Fitzpatrick Associates (1993), "Review of GATT Implications for Ireland", Report to the Department of Tourism and Trade, August.

Government of Ireland (1993), *The National Development Plan 1994-1999.*

Government of Ireland (1994), *A programme for competitiveness and work.*

Hannan and Shortall (1991), "The quality of their education" *ESRI General Paper 153.*

Hashimoto, I. (1981), "Firm specific human capital as a shared investment" *AER Vol. 71,* pp. 475-482.

Higher Education Authority (1993), *First Destination of Award Recipients in Higher Education 1991.*

IAEP, *Learning mathematics.*

IAEP (1992), *Learning science.*

Jones, I. (1988), "An evaluation of youth training" *Oxford Review of Economic Policy,* pp. 54-71.

Lee, G.L. and C. Smith, "Irish engineers: education for emigration?", Routledge.

Lynch, L. (1993), "International comparisons of private sector training", University of Chicago Press.

Lynch, L.M. (1993), "Economics of youth training in the US" *Economic Journal,* pp. 1292-1340.

Lynch, L.M. (1992), "Private sector training and its impacts on the earnings of young workers", *AER,* pp. 299-312.

Mankiw, N.G., D. Romer and D.N. Weil (1992), "A contribution to the empirics of economic growth", *Quarterly Journal of Economics.*

Marris, R. (1983), "The economics of the degree industry", *Birkbeck college discussion Paper 146,* December.

Mcgettigna, D. (1992), "Irish unemployment: a review of the issues" Central Bank of Ireland, Technical Paper 2/RT/92.

Ministry of Finance (1994), *Draft ammended scheme of conciliation and arbitration in the civil service.*

National Centre for Curriculum and Assessment (1990), *Report of the review body on the primary curriculum.*

National Centre for Curriculum and Assessment (1993), *A programme for reform. Curriculum and Assessment Policy towards the New Century.*

National Centre for Curriculum and Assessment (1993), *Education and new technologies of information and communication.*

National Economic and Social Council (1993), *Education and training policies for economic development and growth.*

National Economic and Social Council (1993), *A strategy for competitiveness growth and employment.*

National Education Convention Secretariat (1993), *Background paper for the National Educational Convention.*

National Education Convention Secretariat (1994), *Presentations to the National Educational Convention, Parts 1 and 2.*

National Education Convention Secretariat (1994), *The report on the National Education Convention.*

OECD (1991), *Reviews of National Education Policy, Ireland.*

OECD (1992), *International education indicators: a framework for analysis.*

OECD (1992), *Public educational expenditure, costs and financing 1970-1988.*

OECD (1993), *Education at a glance.*

OECD (1994), *The curriculum redefined: schooling for the 21st century.*

Psacharopoulos, G. (1993), "Returns to investment in education. A global update", *World Bank Working Paper 1067.*

Romer, P. (1989), "Human capital and growth: theory and evidence", *NBER Working Paper 3173.*

Sexton, J.J. (1992), "Human resources and health in Ireland, in Europe: a shared challenge", Government of Ireland.

Shackelton, J.R. (1992), Training too much. A skeptical look at the economics of skill provision in the United Kingdom, *IEA Hobart Paper 118.*

Sheehan, J. (1992), "Education, training and the Culliton report", *UCD Working Paper 92/5.*

Walsh, B.M. (1993), "Labour force participation and the growth of women's employment 1971-1991", *Economic and Social Review,* July.

Chronology of main economic events and policy measures

1993

March

On 4 March, the Central Bank cuts the Short-Term Facility (STF) Rate by 1 per cent to 12 per cent. On 15 March, the STF is cut again – by a ½ point to 11½ per cent. The rate is cut further during the month: on 22 March by ¾ point; and on 29 March by ½ point, thus leaving the STF at 10¼ per cent at the end of the month.

April

The STF is cut three times during April: by ¾ point to 9½ per cent on 5 April; by ½ per cent to 9 per cent on 19 April; and ¼ point to 8¾ per cent on 26 April.

May

The STF is cut by ¼ per cent three times in May – on the 10, 21 and 31 to end the month at 8 per cent.

June

On 23 June, the Central Bank cuts the STF to 7¾ per cent.

July

On 2 July, the Central Bank reduces the STF further to 7½ per cent.

August

Turbulence afflicts the Exchange Rate Mechanism of the European Monetary System, but Ireland, Germany and the Netherlands remain largely unaffected. The normal bands of fluctuation are subsequently widened to +/– 15 per cent.

October

The National Development Plan, setting out the government's proposals for the use of EU Structural Funds for the period 1994 to 1999, is submitted to the European Commission on 8 October 1993 and formally launched on 11 October.

On 26 October, the Central Bank cuts the STF by a further ½ point to 7 per cent.

1994

January

The budget outturn for 1993 brings Exchequer Borrowing Requirement Ir£ 76 million below the target at Ir£ 690 million, or 2.4 per cent of GNP.

The new structure for industrial development agencies, recommended in the Culliton/Moriarty reports, comes into operation – Forbairt deals with indigenous industry, IDA Ireland deals with inward investment while Forfás advises on policy and co-ordinates the approaches and activities of the agencies.

The Central Bank cuts the STF to 6¾ per cent on 10 January.

The 1994 Budget, announced towards the end of the month, sets the Exchequer Borrowing target at 2.7 per cent of GNP, while providing for a number of initiatives intended to reduce the level of unemployment, maintain infrastructural development and improve the tax structure.

February

The government introduces a major new employment initiative, the Community Employment Programme (CEP). The Programme replaced the existing Social Employment Scheme and the Community Employment Development Programme. Provision was made for a significant increase in participants from a base of around 22 000 at end-1993 to a total of 40 000 by end-1994. It is primarily aimed at improving the employment prospects of the long-term unemployed and to that end, the Programme also provides training modules for participants.

The Programme for Competitiveness and Work is launched. This is a national wage agreement between the government, employers and trade unions which commits the parties concerned to the maintenance of wage competitiveness through the moderate evolution of wages.

April

The STF is cut by a further ¼ point on 15 April to 6½ per cent.

May

A further ¼ point cut brings the STF to 6¼ per cent on 16 May.

September

The Council of Ministers agrees that of the twelve EU member states, only Ireland and Luxembourg meet the fiscal performance criteria set out in the Maastricht Treaty.

The European Commission approves the Community Support Framework for Ireland in July and it was launched publicly this month. The Community Support Framework constitutes an agreement between the Commission and the Government of Ireland, based on the proposals in the National Development Plan, on the strategy and priorities for the use of Structural Funds in the period 1994-99.

The Stock Exchange Bill, 1994, is published. The purpose is to regulate stock exchanges and their member firms and fulfil the requirements of EU Investment Services Directive in respect of stock exchanges and their member firms.

The 1994 Labour Force Survey is published. This shows employment growth of over 2½ per cent in the year to April 1994.

December

The new Coalition Government takes office, with agreed policy commitments which include undertakings to restrain nominal growth in current expenditure to 6 per cent in 1995 and real growth to 2 per cent in 1996 and 1997, as well as to maintain adherence to the Maastricht criteria.

1995

January

The 1994 Budget outturn is again better than original expectations, with strong tax revenue buoyancy bringing the Exchequer Borrowing Requirement Ir£ 131 million below target at Ir£ 672 million, or 2.2 per cent of GNP.

February

The first budget of the new administration sets the Exchequer Borrowing target at 2.4 per cent of GNP, citing reward for work, promotion of enterprise and the strengthening of social solidarity as its primary objectives. Principal features include income tax and social insurance reliefs; new and expanded employment schemes; and the focusing of social welfare improvements on children's allowance payments with general rate increases otherwise held to just 2½ per cent (in line with CPI).

The Operational Programme for Industrial Development 1994/99 is launched. The primary focus of the Operational Programme is to build up the competitive capability of indigenous firms so that they can successfully compete in the international market place and thereby lead to long-term self-sustaining employment creation.

March

The interim report on Long-Term Unemployment is published. This advocates a Local Employment Service to assist the long-term unemployed find employment.

The Central Bank raises the STF by ½ point on 3 March, and by a further ½ point on 9 March.

STATISTICAL ANNEX AND STRUCTURAL INDICATORS

Table A. Selected background statistics

	Average 1984-1993	1984	1985	1986	1987	1988	1989	1990	1991	1992	1993
A. Percentage changes from previous year											
Private consumption[1]	3.2	2.0	4.6	0.3	5.0	4.6	7.9	1.3	2.6	2.9	1.2
Gross fixed capital formation[1]	0.0	-2.5	-7.7	-2.1	-2.3	-1.6	13.5	12.8	-8.2	-1.9	-0.5
GDP at market prices[1]	4.4	4.4	3.1	-1.4	5.7	4.3	7.4	8.6	2.9	5.0	4.0
GDP price deflator	3.1	6.4	5.2	5.8	2.1	3.1	4.3	-1.7	1.1	1.3	3.6
Industrial production	6.9	9.6	3.4	2.2	8.9	10.7	11.6	4.7	3.2	9.2	5.6
Employment	0.2	-1.8	-2.5	0.5	0.6	0.3	-0.1	3.3	-0.1	1.2	0.5
Compensation of employees (current prices)	6.9	8.5	7.2	6.8	5.3	5.9	7.1	8.2	6.4	6.8	6.6
Productivity (GDP/employment)	4.2	6.2	5.8	-1.9	5.1	4.0	7.5	5.1	3.0	3.7	3.4
Unit labour costs (compensation/GDP)	2.5	4.0	4.0	8.4	-0.4	1.6	-0.3	-0.4	3.5	1.7	2.5
B. Percentage ratios											
Gross fixed capital formation as % of GDP at constant prices	16.9	20.6	18.4	18.3	16.9	16.0	16.9	17.5	15.6	14.6	14.0
Stockbuilding as % of GDP at constant prices	0.9	1.1	0.9	0.7	0.1	-0.1	1.1	3.0	2.6	-0.2	-0.7
Foreign Balance as % of GDP at current prices	6.0	-0.5	1.6	2.3	5.6	7.6	7.0	5.9	6.5	10.0	13.7
Compensation of employees as % of GDP at current prices	50.5	52.0	51.4	52.6	51.3	50.6	48.3	49.0	50.1	50.3	49.8
Direct taxes as percent of household income	15.0	14.4	14.4	15.2	15.8	16.5	14.6	14.7	14.7	14.6	15.2
Household saving as percent of disposable income	11.0	13.3	10.9	11.4	11.1	9.6	7.4	10.0	10.7	11.8	14.2
Unemployment as percent of total labour force	16.3	15.5	17.4	17.4	17.5	16.7	15.6	13.7	15.7	16.3	16.7
C. Other indicator											
Current balance (billion dollars)	0.5	-1.0	-0.7	-0.8	-0.1	0.1	-0.5	0.1	1.5	2.4	3.8

1. At Constant 1985 prices.
Source: OECD.

Table B. **Expenditure on gross national product, current prices**

Irf million

	1984	1985[1]	1986	1987	1988	1989	1990	1991	1992	1993
Private consumption	9 801	11 384	12 138	12 845	13 811	15 378	15 800	16 607	17 575	18 065
Public consumption	3 067	3 301	3 542	3 575	3 540	3 686	4 082	4 480	4 842	5 167
Gross fixed investment	3 505	3 377	3 456	3 453	3 567	4 277	4 887	4 642	4 661	4 808
Final domestic demand	16 373	18 062	19 136	19 873	20 918	23 341	24 769	25 730	27 078	28 040
Stockbuilding	228	173	118	28	26	275	722	639	–79	–179
Total domestic demand	16 601	18 235	19 254	19 901	20 944	23 616	25 491	26 369	26 999	27 861
Exports	9 770	10 738	10 377	11 855	13 634	16 137	16 116	16 893	18 707	21 871
Imports	9 815	10 397	9 929	10 681	11 921	14 360	14 514	15 072	15 718	17 442
Foreign balance	–45	342	449	1 174	1 713	1 777	1 602	1 821	2 989	4 429
GDP (market prices)	16 556	18 577	19 703	21 075	22 657	25 393	27 093	28 189	29 988	32 290
Net factor income from abroad	–1 639	–1 966	–1 957	–2 112	–2 662	–3 233	–3 131	–2 865	–3 294	–3 727
GNP (market prices)	14 917	16 611	17 746	18 963	19 995	22 161	23 962	25 324	26 694	28 563
Memorandum:										
Composition of stockbuilding										
Agriculture	40	–24	–71	26	80	187	80	34	83	–1
Non-agriculture (incl. EEC intervention stocks)	188	197	189	2	–54	88	642	605	–162	–178

1. Discontinuity in 1985.
Source: CSO, National Income and Expenditure; Department of Finance, Economic Review and Outlook; OECD estimates.

Table C. **Expenditure on gross national product, constant 1985 prices**

Irf million

	1984	1985[1]	1986	1987	1988	1989	1990	1991	1992	1993
Private consumption	10 132	10 598	10 811	12 099	12 636	13 631	13 806	14 161	14 573	14 741
Public consumption	3 242	3 301	3 388	3 223	3 063	3 034	3 212	3 298	3 378	3 415
Gross fixed investment	3 661	3 377	3 317	3 297	3 245	3 684	4 155	3 813	3 741	3 722
Final domestic demand	17 035	17 276	17 515	18 620	18 944	20 350	21 172	21 272	21 692	21 878
Stockbuilding	217	173	132	17	– 15	246	721	642	–39	–177
Total domestic demand	17 252	17 448	17 647	18 637	18 929	20 596	21 894	21 913	21 653	21 701
Exports	10 076	10 738	11 048	12 592	13 708	15 115	16 455	17 313	19 600	21 490
Imports	10 070	10 397	10 982	11 730	12 305	13 873	14 639	14 834	15 639	16 557
Foreign balance	6	342	67	862	1 403	1 242	1 816	2 479	3 961	4 933
GDP (market prices)	17 258	17 790	17 714	19 499	20 331	21 838	23 710	24 392	25 614	26 634
Net factor income from abroad	–1 690	–1 966	–2 089	–2 244	–2 676	–3 028	–3 197	–2 936	–3 452	–3 662
GNP (market prices)	15 568	15 824	15 625	17 256	17 655	18 810	20 512	21 456	22 162	22 972
Memorandum:										
Composition of stockbuilding										
Agriculture	36	–24	–74	24	65	155	75	38	64	–13
Non-agriculture (incl. EEC intervention stocks)	181	197	206	–7	–80	91	647	604	–103	–165

1. Discontinuity in 1985.
Source: CSO, *National Income and Expenditure*; Department of Finance, *Economic Review and Outlook*; OECD estimates.

Table D. **Agricultural output and income**

Ir£ million

	1983	1984	1985	1986	1987	1988	1989	1990	1991	1992	1993
Gross agricultural output [A]	2 555	2 836	2 739	2 721	2 872	3 157	3 377	3 225	3 142	3 363	3 457
Inputs [B]	1 140	1 219	1 262	1 289	1 179	1 229	1 348	1 360	1 372	1 376	1 441
Gross agricultural product[1] [C = A – B]	1 415	1 617	1 477	1 432	1 693	1 928	2 029	1 865	1 770	1 987	2 016
Other expenses less subsidies[2] [D]	284	270	258	290	304	287	303	166	222	144	134
INCOME (self-employed) [= C – D]	1 131	1 347	1 219	1 142	1 389	1 641	1 726	1 699	1 548	1 843	1 882
Annual changes	15.3	19.1	-9.5	-6.3	21.6	18.1	5.2	-1.5	-8.9	19.1	2.1
Volume changes:											
Gross agricultural output	3.3	8.4	-1.5	-1.2	1.2	1.6	2.2	7.4	0.3	5.0	-3.1
Inputs	5.5	-0.4	1.4	6.3	-3.7	0.9	5.5	1.8	0.8	1.1	3.9
Gross agricultural product	1.5	15.8	-3.4	-7.7	5.9	2.3	-1.0	12.9	0.1	7.6	-8.8
Price changes:											
Gross agricultural output	8.5	2.4	-2.0	0.5	4.3	8.2	4.4	-11.0	-3.2	3.0	6.7
Inputs	6.9	7.5	2.2	-4.0	-5.2	3.2	4.0	-0.7	0.3	0.2	0.2
Gross agricultural product	9.9	-1.3	-5.5	5.0	11.7	11.4	5.7	-18.5	-5.2	4.3	10.3

1. At market prices. Gross agricultural product measures value added.
2. Depreciation plus wages and salaries plus land annuities plus agricultural levies less subsidies.
Source: CSO, *Statistical Abstract.*

Table E. **Prices and wages**

Index 1985 = 100

	1985	1986	1987	1988	1989	1990	1991	1992	1993	1994
Agricultural prices	100.0	99.5	103.5	114.4	120.1	106.5	103.1	106.2	113.6	114.8
Livestock price index	100.0	95.6	101.2	113.8	112.4	100.1	96.1	97.2	103.4	105.7
Consumer prices	100.0	103.8	107.0	109.3	113.8	117.6	121.4	125.1	126.9	129.9
Wholesale prices [1]	100.0	97.8	98.4	102.4	108.1	105.1	106.4	107.4	112.4	. .
Industrial prices [2]	100.0	98.8	100.4	104.5	109.5	107.8	108.7	110.5	115.6	116.9
Average hourly earnings in manufacturing	100.0	106.8	113.0	118.2	124.2	131.3	138.1	144.8	153.2	157.0

1. General wholesale price index.
2. Output of manufacturing industry.
Source: CSO, *Statistical Bulletin;* OECD, *Main Economic Indicators.*

Table F. **Household appropriation account**

Ir£ million

	1983	1984	1985	1986	1987	1988	1989	1990	1991	1992
Total personal income	13 523	14 917	15 930	16 857	18 464	19 767	20 958	22 241	23 601	25 262
of which:										
Agricultural	1 286	1 514	1 402	1 332	1 586	1 870	1 976	1 956	1 814	2 124
Non-agricultural employee										
compensation	8 139	8 833	9 465	10 113	10 679	11 309	12 104	13 105	13 956	14 912
Transfers	2 595	2 868	3 129	3 419	3 791	3 917	3 862	4 013	4 490	4 829
Direct taxation	2 665	3 123	3 332	3 625	3 999	4 464	4 325	4 659	4 981	5 329
(as percentage of income)	19.7	20.9	20.9	21.5	21.7	22.6	20.6	20.9	21.1	21.1
Personal disposable income	10 858	11 794	12 598	13 232	14 466	15 303	16 633	17 582	18 621	19 933
Savings ratio (percentage)	18.8	18.2	15.9	14.6	11.2	9.7	7.5	10.1	10.8	11.8
Personal consumption	8 814	9 652	10 598	11 306	12 845	13 811	15 378	15 800	16 607	17 575
Memorandum:										
Real disposable income [1]	12 236	12 382	12 598	12 750	13 625	14 001	14 744	15 363	15 878	16 528
(percentage change)	−1.0	1.2	1.7	1.2	6.9	2.8	5.3	4.2	3.4	4.1

1. Deflated by personal consumption deflator.
Source: CSO, *National Income and Expenditure,* Department of Finance, *Economic Statistics.*

129

Table G. Budgetary position

Irf million

	1988 Esti-mate	1988 Out-turn	1989 Esti-mate	1989 Out-turn	1990 Esti-mate	1990 Out-turn	1991 Esti-mate	1991 Out-turn	1992 Esti-mate	1992 Out-turn	1993 Esti-mate	1993 Out-turn
Current budget												
Expenditure	8 160	8 007	8 150	8 019	8 387	8 421	9 019	9 076	9 648	9 806	10 483	10 519
Revenue	7 035	7 690	7 331	7 756	8 130	8 269	8 775	8 776	9 312	9 360	9 958	10 140
Deficit	1 125	317	819	263	257	152	244	300	336	446	525	379
(as % of GNP)	5.8	1.6	3.9	1.2	1.1	0.7	1.0	1.2	1.3	1.8	1.8	1.3
Capital budget												
Expenditure												
Public capital programme	1 376	1 337	1 392	1 414	1 670	1 661	1 834	1 723	1 907	1 846	2 323	2 131
Other	40	25	30	19	25	23	35	27	45	39	67	125
Total	1 416	1 362	1 422	1 433	1 695	1 684	1 869	1 750	1 952	1 885	2 390	2 256
Resources	1 084	1 060	1 186	1 217	1 503	1 374	1 653	1 549	1 698	1 618	2 149	1 945
Deficit	332	302	236	216	192	310	216	201	254	267	241	311
Exchequer borrowing requirement	1 457	619	1 055	479	449	462	460	501	590	713	766	690
(as % of GNP)	7.6	3.2	5.0	2.3	2.0	2.0	1.9	2.1	2.3	2.8	2.8	2.5
Memorandum:												
Current expenditure[1]	42.3	41.5	38.4	37.7	36.6	36.8	37.2	37.4	38	38.6	36.7	36.8
Current revenue[1]	36.5	39.8	34.5	36.5	35.5	36.1	36.2	36.2	36.7	36.8	34.9	35.5
Public capital programme[1]	7.1	6.9	6.6	6.7	7.3	7.2	7.6	7.1	7.5	7.3	8.1	7.5

1. As a percentage of GNP.
Source: Budget documents; Department of Finance.

Table H. Public expenditure

Ir£ million

	1985	1986	1987	1988	1989	1990	1991	1992	1993	1994
Total public investment	1 695	1 647	1 565	1 335	1 391	1 653	1 687	1 842	2 084	2 379
(as % of GNP)	10.2	9.3	8.3	6.7	6.3	6.9	6.7	6.9	7.3	7.7
Sectoral economic investment	383	394	376	370	445	520	558	608	579	727
of which: Forf/Forbairt/IDA	185	187	213	156	135	120	223	213	250	200
Productive infrastructure	709	638	587	591	651	802	820	897	1 103	1 072
Social infrastructure	603	615	602	374	295	331	309	337	402	645
Central Government current spending	8 682	9 121	9 680	9 641	9 158	9 980	10 743	11 325	12 140	12 956
(as % of GNP)	52.3	51.6	51.0	48.2	41.3	41.6	42.4	42.4	42.5	41.9
National debt interest	1 798	1 792	1 886	1 920	1 932	2 114	2 124	2 085	2 096	2 058
of which: External	(795)	(761)	(804)	(894)	(973)	(1 009)	(1 031)	(923)	(1 021)	..
Current transfers	2 714	2 949	3 074	3 201	3 174	3 339	3 675	4 036	4 384	4 679
Expenditure on goods and services	1 818	1 975	2 053	2 018	2 074	2 233	2 458	2 427	2 562	2 841
Current grants to local authorities	1 937	2 017	2 089	1 800	1 809	1 983	2 185	2 438	2 708	2 968
Memorandum:										
Public capital programme (volume;[2] 1985 = 100)										
Sectoral economic investment	100	100	94	88	100	115	120	128	118	130
Productive infrastructure	100	87	79	76	79	96	95	102	122	114
of which: Roads, etc.	100	99	90	76	89	99	103	110	146	124
Social infrastructure	100	99	95	56	42	47	42	45	52	81
Total	100	94	88	72	71	83	82	88	96	106

1. Department of Finance estimates.
2. Deflator used is that for Gross Fixed Capital Formation.
Source: Budget statements; CSO, *National Income and Expenditure;* Department of Finance, *Public Capital Programme, 1994.*

Table I. **Government revenue**

Irf million

	1985	1986	1987	1988	1989	1990	1991	1992	1993	1994[1]
Taxes on income and wealth	3 557	3 919	4 275	4 821	4 659	5 168	5 602	6 089	6 851	7 255
of which:										
Income taxes	2 105	2 383	2 718	3 046	2 831	3 029	3 222	3 413	3 723	4 049
Corporation taxes	218	258	256	335	303	475	594	739	953	1 140
Social insurance contributions	1 003	1 049	1 109	1 213	1 300	1 420	1 530	1 658	1 801	1 884
Employer	628	661	701	727	783	859	927	995	1 065	1 123
Employee	369	377	407	467	471	508	545	598	663	670
Self employed	–	–	–	22	46	52	58	65	73	91
Taxes on expenditure	2 879	3 024	3 160	3 477	3 828	3 905	3 928	4 188	4 273	4 863
Other revenue	1 043	931	1 051	716	612	713	959	735	776	860
Total income on current account	7 479	7 874	8 486	9 014	9 099	9 786	10 487	11 012	11 900	12 978
(% of GNP)	45.0	44.5	44.8	45.1	41.1	40.8	41.4	41.3	41.7	41.9
Memorandum item:										
Rates paid to local authorities[2]	141	153	170	194	231	239	252	265	280	298

1. Provisional figures.
2. Rates are property taxes.
Source: Budget statements (various issues); CSO, *National Income and Expenditure.*

Table J.   **The relationship between the Exchequer Borrowing Requirement and the Maastricht borrowing target**[1]

Irf million

	1992	1993	1994	1995
Exchequer Borrowing Requirement	−713	−690	−672	−813
Excluding: loan disbursements	−104	−231	−316	−181
loan repayments	150	343	296	214
Net Exchequer Borrowing Requirement	−759	−802	−652	−846
Plus: accruals adjustment, expenditure	−22	−22	−91	−108
accruals adjustment, revenue	18	−68	−2	−
Net Exchequer Borrowing , accruals basis	−763	−892	−745	−954
Plus transactions of off-budget funds:				
Interest paid by exchequer *vs* Central Government				
interest	52	49	11	−
FEOGA negative subsidies	33	58	−61	−50
Gross trading income semi-state bodies	−14	−16	−16	−22
Other transactions	−28	−5	−3	9
Net central government borrowing (−)	−720	−806	−814	−1 017
Net local government borrowing (−)/lending (+)	−1	34	16	−15
Net social security fund borrowing (−)/lending (+)	5	1	−1	−17
Net general government borrowing (Maastricht target variable)	−716	−771	−799	−1 049
Memorandum item:				
As per cent of nominal GNP	26 700	28 575	30 975	33 575
Exchequer Borrowing Requirement	−2.7	−2.4	−2.2	−2.4
Net general government borrowing (Maastricht targt variable)	−2.7	−2.7	−2.6	−3.1
As per cent of nominal GDP	29 887	32 290	35 175	38 375
Exchequer Borrowing Requirement	−2.4	−2.1	−1.9	−2.1
Net general government borrowing (Maastricht target variable)	−2.4	−2.4	−2.3	−2.7

1.   Borrowing is shown as a négative item.
Source: Ministry of Finance.

Table K. **Public sector debt**

Ir£ million

	1985	1986	1987	1988	1989	1990	1991	1992	1993	1994
Net Borrowing[1]	2 239	2 334	1 955	627	519	840	356	764	1 025	385
Government	2 015	2 145	1 786	619	479	462	231	713	690	672
Semi-state bodies	224	189	169	8	40	378	125	51	335	–287
Outstanding debt (year-end)	22 748	26 165	28 477	29 400	29 655	30 216	30 552	31 558	33 901	34 918
Government[2]	18 502	21 611	23 694	24 611	24 828	25 083	25 378	26 344	28 358	29 227
Semi-state bodies	4 246	4 554	4 783	4 789	4 827	5 133	5 174	5 213	5 549	5 691
Interest payments										
Government[3]	1 967	1 989	2 118	2 141	2 141	2 300	2 351	2 355	2 390	2 227
Semi-state bodies	463	506	422	381	397	435	443	460	469	429

1. Includes net borrowing for capital and current purposes by the Government and by the Semi-state bodies.
2. National Debt Statistics from 1982 onwards have been revised as a result of the enactment of the Local Loans Fund (Amendment) Act, 1987 which eliminates circular transfers.
3. Central fund debt services issues including sinking funds and expenses of borrowing.
Source: Department of Finance and Central Bank of Ireland, *Quarterly Bulletin.*

Table L. **Public sector external debt**[1]

Ir£ million

	1985	1986	1987	1988	1989	1990	1991	1992	1993	1994
Gross external borrowing	1 285	1 443	1 073	-82	463	733	663	1 720	710	374
Government	1 098[2]	1 148[3]	1 005[4]	-166[5]	150[6]	342[7]	495[8]	1 518[9]	705[10]	481[11]
Semi-state bodies	127	295	68	84	313	391	168	202	5	-107
Net external borrowing	753	917	475	-674	51	194	5	966	-271	-711
Government	806	812	592	-443	-29	-44	-23	1 008	-60	-388
Semi-state bodies	-53	105	-117	-231	80	238	28	-42	-211	-323
Outstanding external debt(year-end)	10 206	11 570	11 964	11 537	11 231	11 116	11 064	12 284	13 316	13 025
Government	8 114	9 220	9 693	9 498	9 123	8 848	8 859	10 122	11 386	10 978
Semi-state bodies	2 092	2 350	2 271	2 039	2 109	2 268	2 205	2 162	1 930	2 047
Interest payments	987	940	884	869	906	918	935	896	957	1 016
Government	783	716	722	703	736	730	736	710	780	867
Semi-state bodies	204	224	162	166	170	188	199	186	177	149
Memorandum:										
Official external (year-end) reserves	2 272	2 205	2 821	3 161	2 521	2 892	3 256	2 113	4 278	4 041
Net external liability of licensed banks	3 361	3 821	3 578	3 928	3 584	4 393	3 858	2 246	1 029	1 286
Net external banking assets (+)/liabilities (−)	-1 089	-1 616	-757	-767	-1 063	-1 501	-602	-133	3 249	2 755
Foreign holdings of Irish Government securities:										
Net Sales (+ denotes nonresident purchases)[12]	+83	+240	+460	+867	+1 320	+64	+233	-1 809	+1 672	-421
Outstanding[13]	890	1 176	1 800	2 690	3 829	3 892	4 112	2 321	4 047	..

1. Excludes foreign holding of Irish Government Securities which are shown separately in the Memorandums items.
2. Excluding prepayments and renegotiations of £1 222 m.
3. Excluding prepayments and renegotiations of £1 239 m.
4. Excluding prepayments and renegotiations of £946 m.
5. Excluding prepayments and renegotiations of £726 m.
6. Excluding prepayments and renegotiations of £529 m.
7. Excluding prepayments and renegotiations of £499 m.
8. Excluding prepayments and renegociations of £219 m.
9. Excluding prepayments and renegociations of £480 m.
10. Excluding prepayments and renegociations of £672 m.
11. Excluding prepayments and renegociations of £573 m.
12. Gilts and Exchequer bills.
13. Figures refer to gilts and exchequer bills.
Source: Department of Finance and Central Bank.

Table M. **Balance of payments**

OECD basis; US$ million

	1984	1985	1986	1987	1988	1989	1990	1991	1992	1993
Exports, fob	9 423	10 073	12 297	15 537	18 378	20 349	23 319	23 609	27 891	28 465
Imports, fob	9 171	9 451	11 159	12 935	14 550	16 334	19 331	19 421	21 084	20 361
Trade balance	251	622	1 139	2 602	3 828	4 015	3 988	4 188	6 807	8 104
Services, net	-2 077	-2 342	-3 240	-4 005	-5 285	-6 074	-6 515	-5 874	-7 321	-7 267
Balance on goods and services	-1 826	-1 720	-2 101	-1 403	-1 457	-2 059	-2 527	-1 686	-514	837
Private transfers, net	-33	-21	-56	-159	-119	-94	-65	-58	-61	-53
Official transfers, net	839	1 055	1 339	1 466	1 659	1 664	2 655	3 224	3 014	2 820
Current balance	-1 020	-686	-818	-96	83	-489	63	1 480	2 439	3 604
Long-term capital (excluding special transactions)	765	979	1 061	849	-347	-1 212	-2 913	-2 513	-3 935	662
a) Private[1]	1 096	1 070	1 432	-834	271	-799	-2 676	-2 299	-5 076	1 263
b) Official	-331	-91	-371	1 683	-618	-412	-237	-214	1 140	-602
Basic balance	-255	293	243	753	-264	-1 701	-2 850	-1 033	-1 496	4 266
Non-monetary short-term official capital	-2	0	0	0	0	-3	0	-3	1 251	-1 183
Errors and omissions	-189	-362	-1 078	349	347	1 135	2 487	2 177	504	-28
Balance on non-monetary transactions	-446	-69	-835	1 102	83	-569	-363	1 141	259	3 055
Private monetary institutions' short-term capital	412	296	735	-213	441	-333	1 212	-695	-2 298	-1 270
Balance on official settlements	-34	227	-100	889	524	-902	849	446	-2 039	1 785

1. Includes non-monetary short-term private capital.
Source: Direct communication to the OECD.

Table N. **Foreign trade and payments**

	1983	1984	1985	1986	1987	1988	1989	1990	1991	1992	1993
Imports, Irf million	7 367	8 912	9 428	8 621	9 155	10 215	12 284	12 469	12 851	13 195	14 798
Exports, Irf million	6 944	8 898	9 743	9 374	10 724	12 305	14 597	14 337	15 019	16 629	19 656
Trade balance, Irf million	-423	-15	315	753	1 568	2 090	2 313	1 868	2 168	3 434	4 858
Volume of imports (1990 = 100)	63.5	70.0	72.3	74.4	79.1	82.8	93.6	100	100.8	105.6	112.3
Volume of exports (1990 = 100)	51.7	61.2	65.2	67.6	77.4	82.9	92.2	100	105.6	120.1	132.2
Import unit values (1990 = 100)	93.1	102.1	104.5	92.9	92.8	98.9	105.3	100	102.3	100.2	105.4
Export unit values (1990 = 100)	93.6	101.5	104.3	96.7	96.6	103.6	110.5	100	99.3	96.6	103.9
Terms of trade	100.5	99.4	99.8	104.1	104.1	104.8	104.9	100	97.1	96.4	98.6
Official external reserves, Irf million[1]	2 015	2 101	2 272	2 205	2 821	3 161	2 521	2 892	3 256	2 113	4 278

1. At end of year.
Source: CSO, *Statistical Bulletin;* Central Bank of Ireland, *Quarterly Bulletin.*

Table O. **Foreign trade by commodities**

$ million

	Exports, fob								
	1985	1986	1987	1988	1989	1990	1991	1992	1993
SITC Section									
0. Food and live animals	2 354	2 946	3 986	4 412	4 544	4 740	4 892	6 246	5 660
1. Beverages and tobacco	252	307	353	383	422	542	572	642	639
2. Crude materials, inedible, except fuels	456	522	630	802	854	819	758	797	673
3. Mineral fuels, lubricants and related materials	132	99	115	103	103	156	151	172	170
4. Animal and vegetable oils and fats	17	14	15	17	18	18	19	24	26
5. Chemicals	1 460	1 641	1 910	2 435	2 932	3 748	4 253	5 440	5 536
6. Manufactured goods, classified by materials	964	1 186	1 400	1 590	1 638	1 922	1 956	2 150	1 671
7. Machinery and transport equipment	3 084	3 841	5 011	5 846	6 593	7 447	7 124	7 637	8 328
8. Miscellaneous manufactured articles	1 153	1 489	1 943	2 439	2 778	3 379	3 615	4 358	4 030
9. Commodities and transactions not classified elsewhere	527	559	608	710	802	1 026	889	865	2 081
Total	10 399	12 604	15 970	18 736	20 685	23 796	24 229	28 331	28 814
	Imports, cif								
0. Food and live animals	1 060	1 318	1 466	1 625	1 636	1 862	1 985	2 188	1 790
1. Beverages and tobacco	111	130	155	192	198	256	295	352	277
2. Crude materials, inedible, except fuels	316	337	383	429	467	545	506	485	484
3. Mineral fuels, lubricants and related materials	1 196	983	1 007	870	963	1 341	1 227	1 177	1 035
4. Animal and vegetable oils and fats	63	55	56	66	69	66	66	70	80
5. Chemicals	1 176	1 405	1 676	1 958	2 149	2 563	2 744	2 901	2 669
6. Manufactured goods, classified by materials	1 509	1 837	2 147	2 528	2 653	3 231	3 148	3 322	2 524
7. Machinery and transport equipment	3 141	3 638	4 561	5 357	6 591	7 442	7 202	8 010	8 000
8. Miscellaneous manufactured articles	1 163	1 503	1 745	2 047	2 197	2 826	2 999	3 343	2 878
9. Commodities and transactions not classified elsewhere	314	358	419	486	492	583	579	638	1 940
Total	10 049	11 564	13 614	15 558	17 416	20 716	20 751	22 469	21 677

Source: OECD, *Foreign Trade Statistics.*

Table P. **Production structure and performance indicators**

	Per cent share of GDP at factor cost			
	1970	1980	1990	1993
A. Production Structure				
Agriculture and fishing	16.9	11.6	9.7	8.8
Industry	36.2	37.3	37.4	37.2
Distribution, transport et communication	19.0	17.7	19.3	17.1
Public administration and defense	5.8	6.8	5.7	5.9
Other domestic	26.6	31.2	32.1	34.8
Adjustment for financial services	–2.5	–4.5	–4.0	–3.9

	Per cent share of total employment			
	1971	1980	1990	1993
Agriculture, forestry and fishing	25.9	18.3	14.9	12.6
Mining and quarrying	1.0	1.0	0.7	0.4
Manufacturing	20.2	21.3	19.8	19.5
Electricity, gas and water	1.3	1.2	1.1	1.0
Construction	8.0	9.0	6.7	6.2
Services	43.5	48.4	56.7	60.2
of which:				
Transport, storage and communication	5.7	6.1	6.0	6.1
Wholesale and retail trade	16.5	16.4	18.0	–
Finance, insurance and real estate	3.5	5.7	8.5	–
Community, social and personal services	17.0	20.2	24.5	–

	1971	1983	1990	1993
B. Other indicators				
Sectoral composition of fixed asset investment by overseas companies (per cent)	–			
Manufacturing	–	99.7	96.9	97.0
of which:				
Metal and engineering	–	39.0	39.1	42.4
Chemicals	–	9.8	6.2	35.8
Textile	–	3.8	5.8	0.0
Food	–	16.8	3.4	14.0
Non-manufacturing	–	0.2	1.9	3.0
R&D as percentage of GDP	0.78	0.78*	–	–
of which: Government	0.37	0.41*	–	–

*   1981 figures.
Source: CSO, *National Income and Expenditure*; IDA (ida) regions only, grant aided investment only; OECD, *Labour Force Statistics*.

Table Q. **Public Sector**

	1970	1980	1990	1994
A. Budget indicators: general government accounts[1] (percentage of GNP)				
Current receipts	34.7	38.8	37.9	39.0
Non-interest expenditure	29.6	38.5	30.9	32.8
Primary budget balance	5.1	0.3	5.7	3.6
Net interest payments	4.0	6.6	7.8	5.8
General government budget balance	1.1	−6.3	−2.6	−2.6
of which:				
Central	1.4	−5.3	−2.6	−2.6
Local authorities	−0.4	−1.1	0.1	0.1
Social security	0.1	0.1	0.0	0.0
General government debt (gross, per cent of GNP)	68.3	84.4	97.5	90.0*
B. The structure of expenditure and taxation (percentage of GNP)				
General government expenditure	40.0	52.9	38.7	38.5
Current consumption	15.3	20.9	15.1	15.8
Transfers to persons	9.0	12.9	14.1	16.0
Subsidies	4.8	3.8	1.1	1.3
Net interest payments	4.0	6.6	7.8	5.8
Capital formation	4.3	5.9	2.1	2.4
General government expenditure by fonction				
Education	5.1	6.0	4.8	4.8
Transportation	3.4	4.7	2.1	n.a.
Health	4.5	8.0	5.1	5.3
Total tax revenue	30.9	34.4	35.4	36.4
Income tax	8.9	12.6	13.0	14.2
of which:				
Personal	6.2	11.0	11.3	11.0
Corporate	2.7	1.5	1.8	3.2
Social security	2.5	4.9	5.2	5.4
Consumption tax	19.1	16.8	15.0	14.5
Tax rates (per cent)				
Top rate of income tax	35[2]	60	53	48
Lower rate of income tax	−	25	30	27
Corporate tax rate (full rate)	5[3]	45	43	44
Consumption tax rate (standard rate)	25[4]	25	23	21

*   Provisional.
1.   National accounts basis.
2.   Standard rate. A variable surtax was also applied.
3.   Turnover tax.
4.   Wholesale tax.
Source: Department of Finance, OECD.

Table R. Labour market indicators

	1989	1990	1991	1992	1993	1994
A. Labour market performance						
Standardised unemployment rate [1]	15.0	12.9	14.7	15.3	15.7	14.9
Unemployment rate: Male	14.9	12.5	14.2	15.2	15.6	14.8*
Female	15.4	13.8	15.6	15.4	15.9	15.1*
Youth	20.5	17.6	21.8	23.1	25.1	
Share of long term unemployment in total unemployment [2]	45.4	44.8	42.4	42.3	44.3	

	1971	1980	1985	1989	1990	1993
B. Structural or institutional characteristics						
Participation rate [3]: Total	64.6	62.3	61.3	60.3	60.8	59.9
Male	94.8	87.6	85.5	82.7	82.2	78.0
Female	33.7	36.3	36.6	37.5	38.9	41.7
Employment/population (15-64 years)	61.1	57.8	50.8	50.9	52.4	52.0
Average hours worked	–	–	43.5	43.8	43.4	42.0
Part-time work (as per cent of dependant employment)	–	–	8.1	7.5	8.1	–
Wage and salary employees (percentage of total employment)	–	76.3**	76.1	75.7	75.4	76.9
Non wage labour costs [4] (percentage of total compensation)	–	–	–	6.4	6.5	7.1

	1971 / 1961	1979 / 1971	1990 / 1980	1993 / 1980
Average percentage changes (annual rates)				
Labour force	0	1.3	0.4	0.8
Employment: Total	0	1.1	–0.6	–0.1
Agriculture	–3.3	–2.6	–2.7	–2.8
Industries	2.1	1.7	–2.1	–1.3
Services	1.0	2.6	0.8	1.4
of which: Public sector	0.7	1.4	–0.1	–0.5

*   Estimates.
**   1981.
1.   Based on ILO definitions using the *Labour Force Survey*, April.
2.   People looking for a job since one year and more.
3.   Participation rate = total labour force/population group (15-64 years).
4.   Employers' contributions to social security and pensions funds.
Source: Department of Finance; OECD, *Labour Force Statistics.*

BASIC STATISTICS

BASIC STATISTICS:

INTERNATIONAL COMPARISONS

	Units	Reference period [1]	Australia	A
Population				
Total	Thousands	1992	17 489	7
Inhabitants per sq. km	Number	1992	2	
Net average annual increase over previous 10 years	%	1992	1.4	
Employment				
Civilian employment (CE)[2]	Thousands	1992	7 637	3
Of which: Agriculture	% of CE		5.3	
Industry	% of CE		23.8	
Services	% of CE		71	
Gross domestic product (GDP)				
At current prices and current exchange rates	Bill. US$	1992	296.6	1
Per capita	US$		16 959	23
At current prices using current PPPs[3]	Bill. US$	1992	294.5	
Per capita	US$		16 800	18
Average annual volume growth over previous 5 years	%	1992	2	
Gross fixed capital formation (GFCF)	% of GDP	1992	19.7	
Of which: Machinery and equipment	% of GDP		9.3	
Residential construction	% of GDP		5.1	
Average annual volume growth over previous 5 years	%	1992	−1	
Gross saving ratio[4]	% of GDP	1992	15.6	
General government				
Current expenditure on goods and services	% of GDP	1992	18.5	
Current disbursements[5]	% of GDP	1992	36.9	
Current receipts	% of GDP	1992	33.1	
Net official development assistance	% of GNP	1992	0.33	
Indicators of living standards				
Private consumption per capita using current PPPs[3]	US$	1992	10 527	9
Passenger cars, per 1 000 inhabitants	Number	1990	430	
Telephones, per 1 000 inhabitants	Number	1990	448	
Television sets, per 1 000 inhabitants	Number	1989	484	
Doctors, per 1 000 inhabitants	Number	1991	2	
Infant mortality per 1 000 live births	Number	1991	7.1	
Wages and prices (average annual increase over previous 5 years)				
Wages (earnings or rates according to availability)	%	1992	5	
Consumer prices	%	1992	5.2	
Foreign trade				
Exports of goods, fob*	Mill. US$	1992	42 844	44
As % of GDP	%		14.4	2
Average annual increase over previous 5 years	%		10.1	
Imports of goods, cif*	Mill. US$	1992	40 751	54
As % of GDP	%		13.7	
Average annual increase over previous 5 years	%		8.6	
Total official reserves[6]	Mill. SDRs	1992	8 152	9
As ratio of average monthly imports of goods	Ratio		2.4	

* At current prices and exchange rates.
1. Unless otherwise stated.
2. According to the definitions used in OECD *Labour Force Statistics.*
3. PPPs = Purchasing Power Parities.
4. Gross saving = Gross national disposable income minus private and government consumption.
5. Current disbursements = Current expenditure on goods and services plus current transfers and payments of property income.
6. Gold included in reserves is valued at 35 SDRs per ounce. End of year.
7. Including Luxembourg.

	Canada	rtugal	Spain	Sweden	Switzerland	Turkey	United Kingdom	United States
45	28 436	858	39 085	8 668	6 875	58 400	57 998	255 610
29	?	107	77	19	166	75	237	27
.2	1.5	0	0.3	0.4	0.6	2.2	0.3	1
24	12 240	498	12 359	4 195	3 481	18 600	25 175	117 598
.6	4.4	11.6	10.1	3.3	5.6	43.9	2.2	2.9
.7	22.7	33.2	32.4	26.5	33.9	22.1	26.5	24.6
.7	7	55.3	57.5	70.2	60.6	34	71.3	72.5
.9	563.7	84.2	576.3	247.2	240.9	159.1	1 042.8	5 937.3
1	19 823	541	14 745	28 522	35 041	2 724	17 981	23 228
5	536.8	95.9	500.2	143.3	152.8	297.3	941.1	5 953.3
1	19 585	743	12 797	16 526	22 221	5 019	16 227	23 291
1	1.1	3.3	3.3	0.6	1.7	3.7	0.9	1.9
1	18.8	26.2	21.8	17	23.7	23	15.6	15.6
6	6.2	..	6.8	6.2	8	8.5	7.2	7.2
6	6.4	..	4.3	5.9	15.7 [10]	7.6	3	3.7
1	1.4	6.8	6.2	-0.6	1.5	4.6	0.6	0.7
3	12.8	25.3	19.1	14.1	29.7	23.1	12.8	14.5
7	21.9	18.3	17	27.8	14.3	12.9	22.3	17.7
6	49.2	..	..	64.6	35.1	..	42.1	36.7
7	43.7	..	..	59.6	34.7	..	38	31.6
9	0.45	0.36	0.26	1	0.47	..	0.31	0.2
0	11 863	124	8 083	8 907	13 043	3 206	10 397	15 637
7	469	260	307	418	441	29	361	568
6	570	263	323	681	905	151	434	509
7	626	176	389	471	406	174	434	814
6	2.2	2.8	3.9	2.9	3	0.9	1.4	2.3
4	6.8	10.8	7.8	6.1	6.2	56.5	7.4	8.9
1	4.4	..	7.7	7.3	..	..	8.3	2.9
7	4.2	11.2	6	6.8	4.1	66.6	6.3	4.3
4 [7]	134 696	990	64 509	55 980	65 478	14 853	190 103	448 033
8	23.9	21.4	11.2	22.6	27.2	9.3	18.2	7.5
2	7.4	14.5	13.7	4.8	7.5	7.5	7.8	12
3 [7]	122 445	588	99 659	49 916	65 587	23 267	220 994	531 070
6	21.7	35.1	17.3	20.2	27.2	14.6	21.2	8.9
4	6.9	17.4	15.3	4.2	5.3	10	7.5	5.5
7 [7]	8 314	912	33 094	16 454	24 185	4 480	26 648	43 831
1	0.8	5.6	4	4	4.4	2.3	1.4	1

cluded in figures for
fers to the public se
cluding non-resident
s: Population and
Accounts, Vol. I.
Indicators. Forei
Financial Statisti

EMPLOYMENT OPPORTUNITIES

Economics Department, OECD

The Economics Department of the OECD offers challenging and rewarding opportunities to economists interested in applied policy analysis in an international environment. The Department's concerns extend across the entire field of economic policy analysis, both macroeconomic and microeconomic. Its main task is to provide, for discussion by committees of senior officials from Member countries, documents and papers dealing with current policy concerns. Within this programme of work, three major responsibilities are:

- to prepare regular surveys of the economies of individual Member countries;
- to issue full twice-yearly reviews of the economic situation and prospects of the OECD countries in the context of world economic trends;
- to analyse specific policy issues in a medium-term context for the OECD as a whole, and to a lesser extent for the non-OECD countries.

The documents prepared for these purposes, together with much of the Department's other economic work, appear in published form in the *OECD Economic Outlook, OECD Economic Surveys, OECD Economic Studies* and the Department's *Working Papers* series.

The Department maintains a world econometric model, INTERLINK, which plays an important role in the preparation of the policy analyses and twice-yearly projections. The availability of extensive cross-country data bases and good computer resources facilitates comparative empirical analysis, much of which is incorporated into the model.

The Department is made up of about 80 professional economists from a variety of backgrounds and Member countries. Most projects are carried out by small teams and last from four to eighteen months. Within the Department, ideas and points of view are widely discussed; there is a lively professional interchange, and all professional staff have the opportunity to contribute actively to the programme of work.

Skills the Economics Department is looking for:

- *a)* Solid competence in using the tools of both microeconomic and macroeconomic theory to answer policy questions. Experience indicates that this normally requires the equivalent of a Ph.D. in economics or substantial relevant professional experience to compensate for a lower degree.
- *b)* Solid knowledge of economic statistics and quantitative methods; this includes how to identify data, estimate structural relationships, apply basic techniques of time series analysis, and test hypotheses. It is essential to be able to interpret results sensibly in an economic policy context.
- *c)* A keen interest in and extensive knowledge of policy issues, economic developments and their political/social contexts.

d) Interest and experience in analysing questions posed by policy-makers and presenting the results to them effectively and judiciously. Thus, work experience in government agencies or policy research institutions is an advantage.

e) The ability to write clearly, effectively, and to the point. The OECD is a bilingual organisation with French and English as the official languages. Candidates must have excellent knowledge of one of these languages, and some knowledge of the other. Knowledge of other languages might also be an advantage for certain posts.

f) For some posts, expertise in a particular area may be important, but a successful candidate is expected to be able to work on a broader range of topics relevant to the work of the Department. Thus, except in rare cases, the Department does not recruit narrow specialists.

g) The Department works on a tight time schedule with strict deadlines. Moreover, much of the work in the Department is carried out in small groups. Thus, the ability to work with other economists from a variety of cultural and professional backgrounds, to supervise junior staff, and to produce work on time is important.

General information

The salary for recruits depends on educational and professional background. Positions carry a basic salary from FF 305 700 or FF 377 208 for Administrators (economists) and from FF 438 348 for Principal Administrators (senior economists). This may be supplemented by expatriation and/or family allowances, depending on nationality, residence and family situation. Initial appointments are for a fixed term of two to three years.

Vacancies are open to candidates from OECD Member countries. The Organisation seeks to maintain an appropriate balance between female and male staff and among nationals from Member countries.

For further information on employment opportunities in the Economics Department, contact:

Administrative Unit
Economics Department
OECD
2, rue André-Pascal
75775 PARIS CEDEX 16
FRANCE

E-Mail: compte.esadmin@oecd.org

Applications citing "ECSUR", together with a detailed *curriculum vitae* in English or French, should be sent to the Head of Personnel at the above address.

MAIN SALES OUTLETS OF OECD PUBLICATIONS
PRINCIPAUX POINTS DE VENTE DES PUBLICATIONS DE L'OCDE

ARGENTINA – ARGENTINE
Carlos Hirsch S.R.L.
Galería Güemes, Florida 165, 4° Piso
333 Buenos Aires   Tel. (1) 331.1787 y 331.2391
                    Telefax: (1) 331.1787

AUSTRALIA – AUSTRALIE
D.A. Information Services
648 Whitehorse Road, P.O.B 163
Mitcham, Victoria 3132   Tel. (03) 873.4411
                         Telefax: (03) 873.5679

AUSTRIA – AUTRICHE
Gerold & Co.
Graben 31
Wien I   Tel. (0222) 533.50.14

BELGIUM – BELGIQUE
Jean De Lannoy
Avenue du Roi 202
B-1060 Bruxelles   Tel. (02) 538.51.69/538.08.41
                   Telefax: (02) 538.08.41

CANADA
Renouf Publishing Company Ltd.
1294 Algoma Road
Ottawa, ON K1B 3W8   Tel. (613) 741.4333
                     Telefax: (613) 741.5439
Stores:
61 Sparks Street
Ottawa, ON K1P 5R1   Tel. (613) 238.8985
211 Yonge Street
Toronto, ON M5B 1M4   Tel. (416) 363.3171
                      Telefax: (416)363.59.63
Les Éditions La Liberté Inc.
3020 Chemin Sainte-Foy
Sainte-Foy, PQ G1X 3V6   Tel. (418) 658.3763
                         Telefax: (418) 658.3763

Federal Publications Inc.
165 University Avenue, Suite 701
Toronto, ON M5H 3B8   Tel. (416) 860.1611
                      Telefax: (416) 860.1608
Les Publications Fédérales
1185 Université
Montréal, QC H3B 3A7   Tel. (514) 954.1633
                       Telefax : (514) 954.1635

CHINA – CHINE
China National Publications Import
Export Corporation (CNPIEC)
16 Gongti E. Road, Chaoyang District
P.O. Box 88 or 50
Beijing 100704 PR   Tel. (01) 506.6688
                    Telefax: (01) 506.3101

CZECH REPUBLIC – RÉPUBLIQUE TCHÈQUE
Artia Pegas Press Ltd.
Narodni Trida 25
POB 825
111 21 Praha 1   Tel. 26.65.68
                 Telefax: 26.20.81

DENMARK – DANEMARK
Munksgaard Book and Subscription Service
35, Nørre Søgade, P.O. Box 2148
DK-1016 København K   Tel. (33) 12.85.70
                      Telefax: (33) 12.93.87

EGYPT – ÉGYPTE
Middle East Observer
41 Sherif Street
Cairo   Tel. 392.6919
        Telefax: 360-6804

FINLAND – FINLANDE
Akateeminen Kirjakauppa
Keskuskatu 1, P.O. Box 128
00100 Helsinki
Subscription Services/Agence d'abonnements :
P.O. Box 23
00371 Helsinki   Tel. (358 0) 12141
                 Telefax: (358 0) 121.4450

FRANCE
OECD/OCDE
Mail Orders/Commandes par correspondance:
2, rue André-Pascal
75775 Paris Cedex 16   Tel. (33-1) 45.24.82.00
                       Telefax: (33-1) 49.10.42.76
                       Telex: 640048 OCDE
Orders via Minitel, France only/
Commandes par Minitel, France exclusivement :
36 15 OCDE

OECD Bookshop/Librairie de l'OCDE :
33, rue Octave-Feuillet
75016 Paris   Tel. (33-1) 45.24.81.67
                   (33-1) 45.24.81.81

Documentation Française
29, quai Voltaire
75007 Paris   Tel. 40.15.70.00

Gibert Jeune (Droit-Économie)
6, place Saint-Michel
75006 Paris   Tel. 43.25.91.19

Librairie du Commerce International
10, avenue d'Iéna
75016 Paris   Tel. 40.73.34.60

Librairie Dunod
Université Paris-Dauphine
Place du Maréchal de Lattre de Tassigny
75016 Paris   Tel. (1) 44.05.40.13

Librairie Lavoisier
11, rue Lavoisier
75008 Paris   Tel. 42.65.39.95

Librairie L.G.D.J. - Montchrestien
20, rue Soufflot
75005 Paris   Tel. 46.33.89.85

Librairie des Sciences Politiques
30, rue Saint-Guillaume
75007 Paris   Tel. 45.48.36.02

P.U.F.
49, boulevard Saint-Michel
75005 Paris   Tel. 43.25.83.40

Librairie de l'Université
12a, rue Nazareth
13100 Aix-en-Provence   Tel. (16) 42.26.18.08

Documentation Française
165, rue Garibaldi
69003 Lyon   Tel. (16) 78.63.32.23

Librairie Decitre
29, place Bellecour
69002 Lyon   Tel. (16) 72.40.54.54

GERMANY – ALLEMAGNE
OECD Publications and Information Centre
August-Bebel-Allee 6
D-53175 Bonn   Tel. (0228) 959.120
               Telefax: (0228) 959.12.17

GREECE – GRÈCE
Librairie Kauffmann
Mavrokordatou 9
106 78 Athens   Tel. (01) 32.55.321
                Telefax: (01) 36.33.967

HONG-KONG
Swindon Book Co. Ltd.
13–15 Lock Road
Kowloon, Hong Kong   Tel. 2376.2062
                     Telefax: 2376.0685

HUNGARY – HONGRIE
Euro Info Service
Margitsziget, Európa Ház
1138 Budapest   Tel. (1) 111.62.16
                Telefax : (1) 111.60.61

ICELAND – ISLANDE
Mál Mog Menning
Laugavegi 18, Pósthólf 392
121 Reykjavik   Tel. 162.35.23

INDIA – INDE
Oxford Book and Stationery Co.
Scindia House
New Delhi 110001   Tel.(11) 331.5896/5308
                   Telefax: (11) 332.5993
17 Park Street
Calcutta 700016   Tel. 240832

INDONESIA – INDONÉSIE
Pdii-Lipi
P.O. Box 4298
Jakarta 12042   Tel. (21) 573.34.67
                Telefax: (21) 573.34.67

IRELAND – IRLANDE
Government Supplies Agency
Publications Section
4/5 Harcourt Road
Dublin 2   Tel. 661.31.11
           Telefax: 478.06.45

ISRAEL
Praedicta
5 Shatner Street
P.O. Box 34030
Jerusalem 91430   Tel. (2) 52.84.90/1/2
                  Telefax: (2) 52.84.93
R.O.Y.
P.O. Box 13056
Tel Aviv 61130   Tél. (3) 49.61.08
                 Telefax (3) 544.60.39

ITALY – ITALIE
Libreria Commissionaria Sansoni
Via Duca di Calabria 1/1
50125 Firenze   Tel. (055) 64.54.15
                Telefax: (055) 64.12.57
Via Bartolini 29
20155 Milano   Tel. (02) 36.50.83
Editrice e Libreria Herder
Piazza Montecitorio 120
00186 Roma   Tel. 679.46.28
             Telefax: 678.47.51
Libreria Hoepli
Via Hoepli 5
20121 Milano   Tel. (02) 86.54.46
               Telefax: (02) 805.28.86
Libreria Scientifica
Dott. Lucio de Biasio 'Aeiou'
Via Coronelli, 6
20146 Milano   Tel. (02) 48.95.45.52
               Telefax: (02) 48.95.45.48

JAPAN – JAPON
OECD Publications and Information Centre
Landic Akasaka Building
2-3-4 Akasaka, Minato-ku
Tokyo 107   Tel. (81.3) 3586.2016
            Telefax: (81.3) 3584.7929

KOREA – CORÉE
Kyobo Book Centre Co. Ltd.
P.O. Box 1658, Kwang Hwa Moon
Seoul   Tel. 730.78.91
        Telefax: 735.00.30

MALAYSIA – MALAISIE
University of Malaya Bookshop
University of Malaya
P.O. Box 1127, Jalan Pantai Baru
59700 Kuala Lumpur
Malaysia   Tel. 756.5000/756.5425
           Telefax: 756.3246

MEXICO – MEXIQUE
Revistas y Periodicos Internacionales S.A. de C.V.
Florencia 57 - 1004
Mexico, D.F. 06600   Tel. 207.81.00
                     Telefax : 208.39.79

NETHERLANDS – PAYS-BAS
SDU Uitgeverij Plantijnstraat
Externe Fondsen
Postbus 20014
2500 EA's-Gravenhage   Tel. (070) 37.89.880
Voor bestellingen: Telefax: (070) 34.75.778

NEW ZEALAND
NOUVELLE-ZÉLANDE
Legislation Services
P.O. Box 12418
Thorndon, Wellington   Tel. (04) 496.5652
                              Telefax: (04) 496.5698

NORWAY – NORVÈGE
Narvesen Info Center – NIC
Bertrand Narvesens vei 2
P.O. Box 6125 Etterstad
0602 Oslo 6   Tel. (022) 57.33.00
                             Telefax: (022) 68.19.01

PAKISTAN
Mirza Book Agency
65 Shahrah Quaid-E-Azam
Lahore 54000   Tel. (42) 353.601
                             Telefax: (42) 231.730

PHILIPPINE – PHILIPPINES
International Book Center
5th Floor, Filipinas Life Bldg.
Ayala Avenue
Metro Manila   Tel. 81.96.76
                             Telex 23312 RHP PH

PORTUGAL
Livraria Portugal
Rua do Carmo 70-74
Apart. 2681
1200 Lisboa   Tel.: (01) 347.49.82/5
                             Telefax: (01) 347.02.64

SINGAPORE – SINGAPOUR
Gower Asia Pacific Pte Ltd.
Golden Wheel Building
41, Kallang Pudding Road, No. 04-03
Singapore 1334   Tel. 741.5166
                             Telefax: 742.9356

SPAIN – ESPAGNE
Mundi-Prensa Libros S.A.
Castelló 37, Apartado 1223
Madrid 28001   Tel. (91) 431.33.99
                             Telefax: (91) 575.39.98

Libreria Internacional AEDOS
Consejo de Ciento 391
08009 – Barcelona   Tel. (93) 488.30.09
                             Telefax: (93) 487.76.59
Llibreria de la Generalitat
Palau Moja
Rambla dels Estudis, 118
08002 – Barcelona
          (Subscripcions) Tel. (93) 318.80.12
          (Publicacions) Tel. (93) 302.67.23
                             Telefax: (93) 412.18.54

SRI LANKA
Centre for Policy Research
c/o Colombo Agencies Ltd.
No. 300-304, Galle Road
Colombo 3   Tel. (1) 574240, 573551-2
                     Telefax: (1) 575394, 510711

SWEDEN – SUÈDE
Fritzes Information Center
Box 16356
Regeringsgatan 12
106 47 Stockholm   Tel. (08) 690.90.90
                             Telefax: (08) 20.50.21

Subscription Agency/Agence d'abonnements :
Wennergren-Williams Info AB
P.O. Box 1305
171 25 Solna   Tel. (08) 705.97.50
                             Téléfax : (08) 27.00.71

SWITZERLAND – SUISSE
Maditec S.A. (Books and Periodicals - Livres
et périodiques)
Chemin des Palettes 4
Case postale 266
1020 Renens VD 1   Tel. (021) 635.08.65
                             Telefax: (021) 635.07.80

Librairie Payot S.A.
4, place Pépinet
CP 3212
1002 Lausanne   Tel. (021) 341.33.47
                             Telefax: (021) 341.33.45

Librairie Unilivres
6, rue de Candolle
1205 Genève   Tel. (022) 320.26.23
                             Telefax: (022) 329.73.18

Subscription Agency/Agence d'abonnements :
Dynapresse Marketing S.A.
38 avenue Vibert
1227 Carouge   Tel.: (022) 308.07.89
                             Telefax : (022) 308.07.99

See also – Voir aussi :
OECD Publications and Information Centre
August-Bebel-Allee 6
D-53175 Bonn (Germany)   Tel. (0228) 959.120
                             Telefax: (0228) 959.12.17

TAIWAN – FORMOSE
Good Faith Worldwide Int'l. Co. Ltd.
9th Floor, No. 118, Sec. 2
Chung Hsiao E. Road
Taipei   Tel. (02) 391.7396/391.7397
                     Telefax: (02) 394.9176

THAILAND – THAÏLANDE
Suksit Siam Co. Ltd.
113, 115 Fuang Nakhon Rd.
Opp. Wat Rajbopith
Bangkok 10200   Tel. (662) 225.9531/2
                             Telefax: (662) 222.5188

TURKEY – TURQUIE
Kültür Yayinlari Is-Türk Ltd. Sti.
Atatürk Bulvari No. 191/Kat 13
Kavaklidere/Ankara   Tel. 428.11.40 Ext. 2458
Dolmabahce Cad. No. 29
Besiktas/Istanbul   Tel. 260.71.88
                             Telex: 43482B

UNITED KINGDOM – ROYAUME-UNI
HMSO
Gen. enquiries   Tel. (071) 873 0011
Postal orders only:
P.O. Box 276, London SW8 5DT
Personal Callers HMSO Bookshop
49 High Holborn, London WC1V 6HB
                             Telefax: (071) 873 8200
Branches at: Belfast, Birmingham, Bristol, Edin-
burgh, Manchester

UNITED STATES – ÉTATS-UNIS
OECD Publications and Information Centre
2001 L Street N.W., Suite 700
Washington, D.C. 20036-4910 Tel. (202) 785.6323
                             Telefax: (202) 785.0350

VENEZUELA
Libreria del Este
Avda F. Miranda 52, Aptdo. 60337
Edificio Galipán
Caracas 106   Tel. 951.1705/951.2307/951.1297
                     Telegram: Libreste Caracas

Subscription to OECD periodicals may also be
placed through main subscription agencies.

Les abonnements aux publications périodiques de
l'OCDE peuvent être souscrits auprès des
principales agences d'abonnement.

Orders and inquiries from countries where Distribu-
tors have not yet been appointed should be sent to:
OECD Publications Service, 2 rue André-Pascal,
75775 Paris Cedex 16, France.

Les commandes provenant de pays où l'OCDE n'a
pas encore désigné de distributeur peuvent être
adressées à : OCDE, Service des Publications,
2, rue André-Pascal, 75775 Paris Cedex 16, France.

1-1995